Defying Odds:
Empowered through Adversities

From a Teenage Single Mother of Two to a Thriving Career Woman

Marva Hyatt

This work portrays actual events in the life of the author as truthfully as recollection permits. While all persons within are actual individuals, some names and identifying characteristics have been changed to respect their privacy.

ISBN: 979-8-89109-200-6 - paperback

ISBN: 979-8-89109-201-3 - ebook

For requests for speaking engagements, bulk copies, or signed copies, please email Marvahyatt7@gmail.com

Cover designer: Jude Mag-asin

Editor: Margaret A. Harrell, https://margaretharrell.com

I dedicate this book to you, my beloved sons. Only God knows the depth of my love for you. Thank you for being patient when I was learning effective skills to raise you well.

I write to give you deeper insight into how God strengthened me to navigate life challenges while you were young. I thank God for entrusting me with your care. It encourages my heart to see how you have grown into impactful adults and how you touch lives in a profound way.

Contents

Foreword

Children having children—that's how it was described when a teenager dropped out of school in Jamaica in the 1980s. Few of those *child mothers* had the chance of achieving anywhere near their full potential—they were written off without a second chance to rewrite their life *script*. Marva was one of those girls who got a second chance to rechart her path when she entered the Teenage Mothers Project in May Pen, Clarendon, Jamaica.

It has been my pleasure to know Marva Hyatt since 1987 when she registered as a student in the Project. I was the Manager/Counsellor at that time and interacted with her frequently. Eventually, the relationship developed from manager and student to mentor and mentee.

I watched her struggle with the many physical, psychological, social, and spiritual challenges that teen mothers face.

Then gradually, she accepted the role of motherhood, accompanied by the knowledge that being a teen mother is associated with mental and emotional stress. She recognized the reality of her situation—a teen mother without a high school diploma. With that acceptance, a metamorphosis began. I witnessed the changes in her demeanor. Her thoughts centered around this truism: "At this stage in my life, failure is not an option."

From the moment you begin reading *Defying Odds: Empowered through Adversities*, Marva will take you along on her journey, showing you how she defies all the odds while being sustained by her faith.

I'm delighted to have read this book and deeply appreciate the author's courage and grit in telling her life story.

I strongly validate *Defying Odds: Empowered through Adversities* and would like nothing more than to see this book in the hands of many people everywhere.

Utealia V. Burrell

Director of Rural Family Support Organization (RuFamSO)

Prologue

He removed the disposable gloves from his hands, then slowly turned. Headed towards a small sink edging the corner of the tiny room, he concluded his assessment. His tone was stern. "Get dressed," he said abruptly.

His voice echoed in my ears like a shout from the top of an icy mountain somewhere far off, somewhere far out in nowhere. His words replayed over and over, again and again. A vinyl record with a nick, back in the '60s, couldn't have done a better job.

I remember lying, scantily dressed, on a narrow white bed, dazed by his revelation, gazing into the ceiling as it closed down on me at full speed.

"Where are your parents?" he asked.

I heard what he said—the question was plain—but for the life of me, I couldn't understand.

My head veered towards him as he casually washed his hands.

"Get dressed," he reiterated.

"Have you told your parents?" he persisted.

Though his questioning was clear and quite simple, somehow, it rendered me speechless and a little numb. My thoughts raced into outer space. The ceiling lights beamed down on my listless body as I wandered far from Earth, trying to process the magnitude of his revelation.

How on earth could this be?

Surely this is not happening.

He must be wrong!

I am merely fifteen and haven't finished high school yet.

Fear gripped me tightly, almost loosening my limbs from their connective tissues.

How could I ever share this with anyone?

This is a huge embarrassment.

I shuddered as shockwaves pierced my body like tiny needles in an acupuncture room.

I felt the gates of the dam collapse. A million and one unanswered questions flooded my mind—the atmosphere now hushed in deafening silence.

The screeching of the cubicle curtains as they opened jolted me back into the examination room. I shivered, not from the climate but from the thought of my unfortunate situation that had just been laid bare.

"Four months is a bit late, but I can still do something about it."

His words confused me.

"You will need to tell your parents and return," he continued.

I knew what that meant, so I vowed, at that moment, his diagnosis would be a secret never to depart my lips.

I left for home, broken—not even the pitter-patter of rain droplets on my face was able to mask the tears flowing down my cheeks. I bellowed in agony as I plodded half a mile to reach the taxi stand in the bustling town square. I was desperate, alone, and disoriented, making my way along the crowded yet familiar route.

I felt like Alice in Wonderland—lost but in thought. I got into the back of a taxi while other passengers hastily filled the remaining seats. We were all huddled together, and I can recall one woman remarking, "Girl, you're wet!"

It was only then I realized I was drenched from the showers that had now finally disguised my river of tears.

Eight weeks had elapsed from the date I last visited my doctor, and noticeable physical changes had started. Curious neighbours had their suspicions, but my family somehow remained oblivious.

I had no intention of enlightening anyone about my condition. I meant it! The fear of rejection and embarrassment was far too great. I had endless fantasies that the day to reveal this secret would not come. Nevertheless, discreetly I began making the necessary preparations for what was yet to be.

Sometime later, I visited Rose, my older sister. She had requested that I watch over her daughter for a few hours. Rose explained her plans to run some errands along with my mother—Mama—who was also visiting her.

Both of them appeared to be on a mission, as was I—for I had been eyeing her mango tree for some time. The tree sat just a few meters from her back door, my perfect opportunity!

Leaving on foot, Rose and Mama headed in the direction of the old family home, a walk that usually took around ten minutes. I decided to take a stroll around the back as my niece slept comfortably in her cot.

It was scorching outside. The afternoon sun had me craving mangoes, so I grabbed at the chance and helped myself to the big East Indian that was beckoning to me. Much to my disgust, Rose guarded those mangoes like a hen would guard her tender chicks.

I stood directly beneath the tree and scanned the branches with longing eyes. There I saw an alluring golden ripe mango concealed behind some leaves. I looked in the direction that Rose and Mama had set off in, making sure they weren't returning yet.

I had no intention of being caught. I looked once again at the mango and repeated the action a few times, trying to figure out how to make it mine.

As the wind blew, the leaves hid the fruit, then revealed it. This was repeated over and over. It was as if the mango and I were playing *peekaboo* and singing the lyrics:

"Peekaboo, where are you?"

"I'm coming after you," I sang joyously.

"Get me if you can!" the mango seemed to shout back.

Surely I can climb this tree. Only the sighting of a green lizard will stop me from coming for you, I thought.

One, two, three, and up the tree I went, swinging from branch to branch. Perched comfortably on one of its sturdy branches, I stretched out a hand while holding tightly onto a limb with the other until I laid hold of the mango.

I separated it gently from its stem and grasped it firmly.

"Mission accomplished!" I exclaimed.

The mango was ripe—just the way I liked it. I sank my teeth into its firm, succulent skin, and soft, juicy flesh. Sweet yellow juice oozed down my chin and hand. Leaving the seed—bare, dry, and almost white—I devoured it!

The branch swayed to and fro in the wind, and I was mesmerized by the cool atmosphere in the tree, which had leaves as numerous as the sand on a seashore.

Bringing my bliss to a halt, my mother appeared under the tree shortly thereafter.

"Marva, how did you get up there?" she asked sternly and frighteningly. "Please come down and be careful not to hurt yourself."

Given her warning tone, I suspected I might be in trouble. Carefully climbing down, I planted my feet on the ground, taking care not to expose my abdomen.

"Marva, how many months pregnant are you, and who is the father?" my mother asked.

Anxiety gripped my whole body. I was stunned. I shuddered. The moment I dreaded had arrived. I wanted the earth to open up and swallow me! I contemplated running, but my legs were weak. I could only stand. Maybe I had gotten some sort of energy from the mango, but my legs should not have been working.

"How far along are you, Marva?" she questioned with an eerie calmness.

"Six months," I whispered sheepishly.

The interrogation continued as mixed emotions played in her eyes. I imagined the sheer shock and disappointment that must have gripped her. She was confirming not only that her daughter was pregnant but also that I was quite advanced.

I began recollecting my doctor's instructions to inform my parents and return to him. I was four months pregnant then. Although I did not want the pregnancy, I refused an abortion. Knowing my mother would not support any decision to terminate the pregnancy either; I was between a rock and a really hard place. What will happen now?

Unbeknownst to me, my sister, Janet, had found some items of baby clothing I had hidden in the ceiling of a room in our house. I had no idea Janet and I were using the same hiding place. Apparently, a little plan was concocted and set in motion.

Aye caramba, the vicissitudes of life!

Janet discussed her suspicions with Rose and Mama. This led them to conclude I was pregnant. Sometime later, I discovered that the mission Rose went on earlier that day was to show Mama the baby clothes. I called it a fact-finding mission.

The truth is, my mother, having invested all she possibly could in my education, had high hopes for me. As a vendor at the local market, she worked very hard to make ends meet—it was tough. Nevertheless, she managed.

I'm still unable to figure out how, but she enrolled me in a private school on her very limited income. I felt I at least owed it to her to do well in school and obtain a solid education.

Now her hope for a bright future was dashed. What she could not have been aware of at that time was my resilience—my ability to bounce back. She did not know the strength of my faith in the enabling power of God to turn my life around. Unaware of any school dropout who managed to turn her life around after becoming a teen mum, she thought that was the end of my journey.

In retrospect, I made sense of my mother's grave disappointment. It is well-researched that teenage mothers, compared to older mothers, are less likely to finish their education, more likely to raise their child or children alone, live in poverty, misuse drugs and alcohol, be dependent on social welfare, and have a higher risk of mental health problems.

While these outcomes are frightening, I am here to tell you that this does not have to be your story. It does not have to be the way your story ends or the way your life turns out because, with God's help, you can defy the odds.

The Bible is filled with promises that remind us of the love and mercies of God and His enabling power to transform lives. His power enables us to overcome self-defeating behaviour. The Psalmist says, "The Lord is gracious and full of compassion, slow to anger and great in mercy. The Lord is good to all, and His tender mercies are over all His works" (Psalm 145: 8–9, NIV). I am a testament to this fact.

Now journey with me as I share how God empowered me to navigate through extremely difficult situations during not just one but two early teen pregnancies to become a police officer and later a social worker.

Part One—The Journey

If you are going through hell,
keep going.

–Winston Churchill

Sometimes it's the journey that
teaches you a lot about your
destination.

– Drake

Chapter 1
Tough Break

Always remember that your present situation is not your destination. The best is yet to come.

—Zig Ziglar

Growing up on the Caribbean island of Jamaica, my family was large but significantly disadvantaged. My mother was poor, and formal education had somehow eluded her—my father was a delinquent. Our perforated, zinc-roofed three-roomed house had some windowpanes missing or broken, similar to the spirit of the household.

The doors lacked secure locks, so we improvised by using a tablespoon or dinner fork to replace the missing bolt, which was the only means of securing each door. The slightest wind at night could easily have compromised the bolts. We lived without electricity or running water.

Our light sources were kerosene lamps, lanterns, and open-flame bottle torches. We fetched water from a distant fire hydrant by using push carts or transporting it in buckets on our heads, using a piece of soft cloth wrapped in a circular pattern as a buffer between our heads and the bucket. We stored the water in large drums or plastic barrels outside the house.

The pit latrine was my usual place of solitude, and newspapers were the special loo rolls. We bathed in small bath pans in one of the open rooms under construction.

I can still remember the coal stove on which we cooked some delicious meals. It was challenging to get the fire started during the rainy months, as the stove and coals were often saturated by heavy showers, but once we did, the meals we cooked were worth the effort.

The kitchen is still etched in my mind. Being situated in one of the unfinished rooms outside, it was roofless, and during late dinner preparation, the stars and moon enhanced the torchlight, illuminating the area. These conditions persisted throughout my childhood.

My parents tried desperately to extend the house, but the unfinished building stood the test of time, remaining that way for years.

My mom had many children. I recall her saying casually to me one day, "You are the sixth child out of twelve, and everything that I experience, you will experience half of it."

On close examination of her life at that time, I saw the impact of poverty, hunger, suffering, parental conflict, and sibling rivalry, among many other struggles. I was determined to rise above hardship. Education would be my way out.

When I cultivated a love for reading, my mother bought me Christian books and magazines. At night, immersing myself in the Bible stories, I watched the kerosene oil disappear slowly from the lamp, and the wick became shorter and shorter as I sat at the dining room table.

As the minutes turned into hours and the hours phased into midnight, the Home Sweet Home lampshade got progressively darker. For Bible stories, I had an insatiable appetite, and I fell in love with the main character, the man Jesus Christ. I wanted to do the things He said we should do so we would live with Him forever in heaven.

None of my family members attended church, although there was a huge church located in our lane—the biggest building then and remains so today. It had a large congregation, with spirited singing each Sunday morning that echoed across the community.

I wanted to go to church to learn more about God, but I wanted to go to one held on Saturdays. I did not know of any.

One day I asked my mother if she knew where any Saturday church was.

"Why Saturday?" she asked.

The Bible said we should remember the Sabbath day to keep it holy, and I wanted to keep all God's commandments.

I could see that my mother was happy about my interest in spiritual matters.

"Yes, there is an elderly couple living on the next street behind ours who attend Saturday church. I will ask them if they could bring you with them," she replied happily.

It was not many days afterwards that I started attending church with the elderly couple. I met other children at church, and I loved my newfound faith and friends.

I did not understand much about Christian doctrines and teachings, but I understood the basics very well. That is, God made a perfect world with everything in it, including the first two human beings, Adam and Eve. They disobeyed God; therefore, they sinned.

All who sin deserve to die, but Jesus Christ came from heaven and died on the Cross for us instead. He was raised from the dead and went back to heaven. He promised to come back and take us to heaven to live with Him forever if we obey His commandments. I wanted to be obedient. I wanted to go to heaven.

At the age of ten, I sat for qualification for high-school entrance—the Common Entrance Examination. I went on to Clarendon College, one of the top high schools in my region. At that time, I was the only child of my parents who went to high school. In fact, I was the only child in the lane where I grew up who went to high school.

My baptism at twelve was a big moment for the family. My mother and siblings were excited. I was a model child in my community, the kind which most parents dream of. I was quiet and disciplined, and my future looked promising. I was the pride of the family—the hope of the future. I was so excited about this journey. I believed I would be the one to make my family proud, but this did not materialize.

Having a toxic marriage, my parents often argued and fought. My father had other relationships and children outside his marriage, which was one reason for the marriage breakdown. I felt my siblings and I were caught in the middle of an ongoing battle.

By the time I started high school, my father no longer lived in our home, and he rarely supported us. This meant that Mama had to be both mother and father. She worked tirelessly to provide food and other basic needs. My siblings and I were only two years apart. My mother, the glue that held the family together, was obviously struggling to cope.

Eventually, my parents divorced. As a result, my mother had new relationships, which produced my five younger siblings. Over time, my mother took my half-siblings and went to live with their father—leaving me and the rest of my father's children at home. I was the youngest of that set.

My mother had seven children by my father, two of whom died in unfortunate circumstances of fire and unexplained illness prior to my mother moving out. This had a profound impact on the family, who, looking back, were in deep grief, which drove my parents further apart.

Consequently, the family disintegrated like withering petals in the scorching summer sun, and the wind carried off the petals where it blew.

When my mother moved out, I was only thirteen. My absent father continued his delinquency—and neither parent prioritized my education. In her defence, my mother had no money.

I felt I had to at least awaken my father's sense of responsibility for my education. Therefore, on school mornings, immaculately dressed in my uniform—a sea blue tunic and a white blouse, I walked to the house where he lived with another woman—about a mile away.

I was hoping that seeing me in my uniform might impress him to give me money for lunch and bus fare—for that day, at least. Otherwise, I would have to once again skip school.

Needless to say, most mornings, it was a wasted journey. I received no lunch money. As you might imagine, it was usually a painful walk to get back home, knowing I would miss school again. Often my eyes flooded with tears as I agonized over when my situation would improve.

Sometimes I would watch sorrowfully as Carol Tours—the large capacity school bus passed me by.

I wanted to go to school so badly but could not. It was about fifteen miles from home, and I would have walked if it were practicable.

Some days when I managed to get to school, I had no lunch money or bus fare to return. So instead of focusing on my learning, I would fret about how to wrangle a ride back. Pauline, my best friend, shared her lunch with me sometimes and gave me a bus ticket on occasion.

As a result, my attendance declined significantly. By the time I reached fourth form (year ten), I had quit school, and my whole world changed at that crucial stage: the year we started preparing for final exams, by which we would advance to fifth form.

At age fifteen, I had a boyfriend, Daniel, whom I met at home. His older sister was dating my eldest brother, and he and his sister visited us regularly at home.

On one of their visits, when I was studying at the dining table, he became curious.

"What are you doing?" he asked.

"I'm practicing math," I told him.

"I love maths. It's my favorite subject," he replied.

Mmm, interesting, I thought.

"What type of math are you doing?" he probed.

"Simultaneous and quadratic equations."

"Ah, we just covered that topic in class. Do you know how to do them?" he asked.

"Quadratic equations. They are difficult, and no, I don't fully understand how to do them," I told him.

"Can I see it? Maybe I can help you," he responded quickly.

I took his offer gladly. Soon Daniel was teaching me formulas for equations, encouraging me to memorize them, as on final exams, the formulas are not given.

We worked through some exercises, and I aced them. I saw that he enjoyed teaching me. As we giggled and chatted, I realized that what was once a mountain was now a plain. Finally, I understood how to do simultaneous and quadratic equations. What a weight off my shoulders.

Daniel made learning fun. And it made me hope I might catch up with my schoolwork and, somehow, the following year, sit for my final exams.

As my newfound friend and his sister began visiting our home frequently, our friendship grew. He took a keen interest in my learning and impressed me with his knowledge and teaching skills, although, like me, he was a student.

It was evident, as I grew fond of him, that the feeling was mutual. To be frank, I felt happy I had a personal maths tutor, as it were, and was catching up on lessons I missed at school.

Daniel knew that no parents lived at our home but not that I attended school so infrequently and why. With his sustained attention to my learning, I felt happy that, at last, someone was showing an interest in my education.

We chatted and laughed a lot, debating which of our high schools was better, especially in sports. At the time, Daniel's school, Vere Technical, was famous for producing world-class athletes—still is to date—and my school was famous for the football championship and national school challenge quiz competition.

For many hours, I laughed my sorrows away. All the while, I felt deep feelings growing in my heart. I figured it was what they called love. I did not know what love really was. Nobody had taught me.

Love and sex were topics that were out of bounds for kids in my family. Every time a new sibling arrived, my mother concocted a story for us about where the baby came from. Like, she bought them from the shop or something equally far-fetched.

Later, when a new sibling arrived every other year, we said, "Mama, you are to stop now. You can't afford to take care of us all." She said, "I'm having my lot out!"

After all, she did not really purchase the baby from the shop, eh?

Anyway, in my eyes, Daniel was a handsome lad, and I felt I'd found my prince. I remembered he had an Oxford English Dictionary, and on the top of every other page, he had written my first name. His first name was on the alternate pages. So, taken together, our names were on every page. That told me he had been thinking deeply about me. He didn't know I saw it.

It did not take long to find out that I was not going to school. I trusted Daniel and told him what was happening at home. Sometimes, I did not have food or basic toiletries. My mother had no money, her thriving business had collapsed, and she stopped selling in the market.

Daniel pitied my condition and started sharing his lunch money so I could return to school. He even shopped for my personal items, including sanitary pads. He ensured I did not run out. This meant a lot to me because, for the first time, it meant I did not have to worry about food and personal items.

He even cooked my dinner at his house and dropped it off in the evenings. If I did not get home from school by the time he arrived and no one was at home, he hid it in a secret place, so no one would find it and eat it. Basically, he took up where my parents left off.

Like me, Daniel had absent parents. His mother had immigrated to North America—though still supporting him financially. But he had more support from his siblings than I did from mine.

One evening during one of his visits, Daniel popped out from his pocket a neatly folded letter. It was not in an envelope, and the way it was folded sent a message. I felt my heart skip a beat. He handed it over to me, asking that I read it after he left. I was eager to open it but managed to contain my curiosity. For the first time, I wanted his visit to end sooner than usual.

As he left, I quickly opened the interlocking, folded, perfumed letter, whereupon my eyes beheld these words: "Will you be my girlfriend?"

I felt like shouting at the top of my lungs, YES! YES! so he could hear and return. I felt special that Daniel would now be my prince charming. He became the apple of my eye.

Daniel told me when we got older, we would get married and live together forever. I believed him. I loved him, and he and his siblings became my source of strength. I started spending weekends at his house. His siblings, being adults, loved me and treated me as family.

Everything went well for a while. I started attending school more regularly and achieved high scores academically.

On reflection, we were two high-school students from broken homes looking for love, affection, and a better understanding of life.

However, instead of the high-school graduation I was dreaming of, I became pregnant. Five days after my sixteenth birthday, I was the mother of a son—my first child.

Tough break!

During my pregnancy, our relationship turned sour. When I found out I was pregnant at four months, Daniel struggled to accept it. Why had I taken so long to tell him? He wanted to know.

The fact was, I knew nothing about the pregnancy. Not until a routine checkup for school purposes. That was when I found out! During the routine checkup, the doctor discovered it.

I did not miss my period. I noticed slight physical changes but thought my body was just developing. In my mind, I was still a virgin, although we had *experimented* with sex.

How naïve I was! To this day, it still baffles me.

Daniel started to distance himself, denying he was the father. As a result, my whole world fell apart, and I became afraid to tell anyone.

I dreaded condemnation from my family and the community.

My family had warned me about having a boyfriend and admonished me to *hold my head up* despite having no parents at home.

Even though our family was fragmented, I wanted to keep the family honor, not add to what was already a difficult situation. I expected I would have to be the one to lift the family out of poverty.

Fearful of the added responsibility pregnancy would bring everyone, I was afraid they would turn me away. So, I kept the secret meticulously until I was six months advanced—two months after I knew.

At full term, I delivered a fit and healthy, bouncing boy baby at the local hospital. He had an average birth weight, and I thanked God I had no medical complications or suffered any lasting health issues.

It is well known that babies born to teen mothers are at an increased risk of being born premature or with dangerously birth weight.

Research suggests a low-birth-weight baby can have many serious health problems, and I feared this might be my situation, although I had my antenatal checkups.

My motherhood role began, and I was discharged to the care of my older sister.

One week after my son's birth, Daniel immigrated to North America. He never kept in touch. However, not long after arriving in North America, he was involved in a very serious car accident and was in a coma for many days.

He survived but suffered a degree of permanent memory loss of his past. I empathized with his condition. In addition, it was a setback for my son and me. I had many questions I wanted answers for.

I wanted closure to that difficult period of my life. I wanted to know why he had denied paternity.

Was it because I was underage? Why did he switch at a time I needed him most? Was it to protect himself?

For many years any meaningful conversation with Daniel about his reason for denying paternity proved impossible.

It was so absurd! I thought he was dreaming and would wake up soon.

How could Daniel deny that he was the father? Everyone knew he was the only person with whom I'd had any form of relationship.

Frankly, I was too embarrassed to tell anyone the truth about the situation.

Years later, when I sought answers, Daniel told me he could not remember the sequence of events. But he remembered being afraid of backlash from my family, particularly my eldest brother.

Whatever his reasons, it meant that my son grew up without him in his life—which was sorrowful for not just my son but also me.

Like my mother, I now had to be a mother and father to my son. During those times, I felt like the world had closed in on me. No one cared about me, and I was left to fend for myself and my child. My family told me I was no good and that I should go and find my child's father.

The odds seemed continually stacked against me.

At the time of my son's birth, I barely knew how to care for myself, much less a child.

Tempted to give up many times, I had to take things day by day. But somewhere deep inside, I believed God was sustaining me because I had a strong sense that I could not give up. I had to keep going for my son and me.

I often did not have food to eat and could not provide for my child's basic needs. My life seemed to be going downhill rapidly. Nothing was working in my favor. I felt abandoned and rejected; nevertheless, I still had my goal in mind—to become a civil servant.

At the time, I was unsure which government department I wanted to work with, but I was determined. So, I had to pass a milestone to get me there, and that was to return to school and take my final exam.

I also learned of an initiative called Teenage Mothers Project (TMP), launched by the University of the West Indies—Mona, Jamaica. It targeted girls at risk of dropping out of the school system because of early pregnancy and opened around the time of my first son's birth. It provided the participants with education, counseling, and child-care services.

Excitedly, I learned of this initiative in the parish where I grew up. In this intervention, set up by the Bernard Van Leer Foundation of the Netherlands, I saw the promise of a brighter future.

The project aimed to decrease the number of teen pregnancies and their frequency in and around my area, addressing the growth and training of teen mums, decreasing the likelihood of repeat pregnancy, and thereby improving the life opportunities of the children.

I was overjoyed that TMP assisted first-time mothers and first-time mothers-to-be with services suited to my needs.

The babies were placed in a stimulating daycare centre, supervised by caregivers trained specifically by the project. In this environment, the children felt safe and confident.

Some of the criteria to join the program were that you had to have dropped out of school, live with your family, and be pregnant before reaching your seventeenth birthday.

Determined to utilize this opportunity to turn my life around, I fit all the criteria. The intervention lasted approximately eighteen months.

At the time we joined, the mothers and mothers-to-be ranged from ages twelve to sixteen. We hailed from different academic backgrounds—primary to high school. From different family backgrounds also.

Being accepted into the program meant that my son and I would have daily food, and I could continue my education and achieve my goal of becoming a civil servant. Therefore, it looked like things were turning around. I was overjoyed.

TMP was my lifesaver.

I was making good progress academically and socially. I went there daily and established some good friendships with other mums and mums-to-be. We chatted about our joys and sorrows, dreams and aspirations for ourselves and our children.

I was happy again.

There was a real sense of family bond. I felt valued, loved, and appreciated. And I believe that was the sentiment of all my peers.

Hosted in a former dwelling house, the project, therefore, felt a lot like a home. The managers and staff were like our mothers and aunts, and we were siblings.

I felt connected, felt I belonged. The sisterhood developed in the program filled the deep void of love and affection that was within me. It filled this longing left by my biological family.

I looked forward to going there each day, even if it meant I had to bum a ride to get there. I did not miss a day. We were reimbursed bus fares, but sometimes I used my bus fare to buy food or toiletries.

We assisted in some areas of operation of the project, such as shopping, cooking, serving, doing the dishes, cleaning up, and preparing for class. These chores equipped us with life skills. To this day, doing household chores is my favorite hobby.

At the end of each week, we were given food parcels, chiefly made up of a small measure of flour, rice, cornmeal, milk powder, and sugar. This was a big help as it meant we only needed a protein source for a meal.

For me, the protein source was ackees from a faithful fruit tree by the wayside or chicken back (the boney portion of the chicken) purchased at the local market or a corner shop. I could not afford the meatier portion of the chicken.

I used the sugar to make a simple, refreshing beverage known as *sugar and water*, or if I managed to find limes from a tree at the back of our yard, then I made lemonade.

As I progressed at TMP, one of the project managers told me of her plan to adopt my son and me, taking us to live with her in Kingston. She even planned to enroll me in a teachers' training college.

I was over the moon. Life had just gotten exciting!

The lady was elegant with a wealthy appearance, and I wondered if I could meet her expectations. She was refined and dignified, often addressing us (the teenage mums or mums-to-be) on social etiquette and decorum. She desired that we should not just live but thrive, despite our label of teenage mums. To her, excellence was everything.

I now had a vision for my life to rise above poverty and hardship. I again began to dream of my family, especially Mama, having a better life.

I was preparing to sit my final exams, and my family became happy for me again, and I believed they were genuinely hopeful.

After all, I'm the *Child of Promise*.

Even though my family was poor, I did not realize how disadvantaged we were because that was the only life I knew. Moreover, life was almost the same for the other families of the rural community in which I grew up.

Good role models were few and far between. Gun crimes regularly plagued the community, teen pregnancies were prevalent, and family dramas played out in the street or the neighbors' yards.

I yearned for love and affection, warmth and tenderness—needs that were largely unmet. I was not confident I could open up about my true feelings to my parents or siblings. I felt that if I opened up, they would think me rude—question whether I had lost my mind.

On reflection, today, as a matter of fact, I realize we were all going through the same emotional turmoil.

When my mother lived at home, my dad was busy procreating with other women. As a result, I have many siblings by my father's side, some of whom—up to the time of writing this book—I haven't met.

It's my desire to locate them and plan one big reunion, or rather union because we've never met. I would love to do this before my father or any of us goes into that deep sleep we call death.

In order to keep a positive mindset, I reminded myself daily that teenage pregnancy was not the end of my life. I must turn my pain into gain. I told myself that my *failure*, or so it seemed, was "a detour, not a dead-end street," as coined famously by Zig Ziglar.

I learnt that in order to move forward, I had to do two things:

1. Change how I see God

2. Change how I see myself

Firstly, I adjusted how I see God; that is, to have a deeper understanding of His character—knowing He is compassionate and merciful, slow to get angry, and filled with unfailing love (Psalm 103:8, NLT). God loves me so much that He sent Jesus Christ from heaven to earth to die for me. And it's the same for every one of us.

I kept running away from God because I thought I was so sinful. I had a child out of wedlock, I had backslidden, and the Christian life was hard to follow. An adjusted view brought me to the revelation that I needed God's help.

A corrected view enabled me to see that my situation was dire and I needed divine intervention. I needed to tap into a source outside myself, and that was God. He has infinite power to turn things around.

Although I was not going to church and reading my Bible, *I believed in God's limitless power to give life to dead situations.*

Matthew 19:26 KJV says, *...with God, all things are possible*. I believe He is most glorified when He brings to pass a situation that had seemed impossible to us humans. I had faith in God that He would create a way for me to achieve my life goal—showing himself merciful and silencing all my critics.

I wanted a *good job* and a career, and I was willing to put the work in to redeem time and achieve it.

I did not know how it would happen, but I knew deep down that God would make a way for me. He is God, full stop.

In the scriptures, God wrought powerful miracles for ordinary people. I was an ordinary girl who lost her way and faced huge difficulties.

God helped me to *defy the odds.*

Secondly, I adjusted my vision of myself. That is my outlook on life. Failing to adjust my vision would have given me a twisted view of myself—having been told constantly that I was a failure and would come to nothing good.

I had to get rid of those negative perceptions—cast them out of my head. Frankly, this meant blanking some people out of my life.

Zig Ziglar is credited with saying, "Don't let negative and toxic people rent space in your head. Raise the rent and kick them out!"

Negative people will never help you rise above your situation but only keep pulling you down.

I had to be gentle with myself and love and forgive myself. This enabled me to have the right attitude toward myself and others.

I told myself I was born for a reason. I have a right to be here; I am not an accident. I have a place in this world, and no one was going to occupy my headspace because of their skewed view of me.

I wasn't arrogant. I accepted that I messed up, but so did thousands of other girls around the world.

TMP came looking for girls like me—to give us a second chance and to help fulfil the reason we exist.

I thank God for TMP's generosity. I believe God developed that program to give me focus and direction.

It was not a coincidence that the project came into being just at the time of my son's birth.

It's like Jonah and the fish in the Bible. The fish did not just happen to be near the boat when Jonah was thrown overboard. The fish was divinely positioned to receive Jonah and redirect him. The TMP initiative was divinely orchestrated. It was meant to prepare and redirect me.

Takeaways

These days, accessing information is much easier than when I was a teen. The Internet is awash with useful information on parenting: for example, websites such as https://kidshealth.org/ are helpful. Additionally, in the book *Child Guidance,* by Ellen G. White, she gave guidance on parenting that I believe is pertinent to mention here:

1. Be equipped for parenting

Many who are tasked with raising children are, more often than not, without knowledge of what their physical needs are. They lack knowledge of the basics of good health or what proper development truly means. It is highly unlikely that you'll find them proficient in the care of their children's mental health or spiritual upbringing.

2. Don't leave out God

Without making God's words the rule of their lives, parents cannot properly fulfil their responsibilities. The Bible should be used as a guide. If children are trained in accordance with the instructions it provides–the manual of life–parents are not only placing their child on the right path but also educating themselves in their divine responsibilities.

3. A mother's role is key

The first teacher of any child is its mother—except in extenuating circumstances, I might add. During the impressionable years, when a vast majority of its development takes place, the child's education is mostly in her hands. She has first dibs. This is an important responsibility, above all else.

4. Father, your child needs your guidance

Fathers have an equal responsibility to that of a child's mother as it relates to the teaching of a child from conception to adulthood. It is pivotal that both parents are prepared adequately before taking up this mantle and that they have sufficient knowledge of the foundation of perceptual, motor, and physical development of a child and moral training.

5. Lead by example

Children learn a lot about how to act by observing their parents. An example is the most effective teacher, I believe. You are to model the traits you wish to see in your children: respect, friendliness, honesty, kindness, and tolerance. Exhibit unselfish behavior. Remember the golden rule, 'Do unto others as you would have them do unto you.' A child's environment has a significant impact on shaping their behaviour. By cultivating and maintaining the appropriate environment, their behaviour and character may be influenced positively. Be a model parent!

6. Love your child unconditionally

Love must be the foundation of parenting. Every act should be motivated by love, even in disciplining your child. Love must be cultivated, nurtured, practised, and demonstrated until it is recognized, believed, appreciated, and treasured.

Parents are responsible for correcting and guiding their children. But how you express your corrective guidance makes all the difference in how a child receives it. When disciplining your child, avoid criticizing, blaming, or fault-finding. These affect their self-esteem and can lead to resentment. Instead, try to nurture and encourage, ensuring you communicate to them in words and actions that you love them, regardless.

Chapter 2
Oops, I Did It Again

You never make the same mistake twice. The second time you make it, it is no longer a mistake. It is a choice.

—Lauren Conrad

The long summer holiday (eight weeks) came. Like regular schools, TMP shut its doors. Teachers and staff would refresh themselves from the tiring but rewarding work of caring for our children and us.

My life was far from a theme park, but I looked forward to fun—happiness and adventure—a much-needed break from my routine. I had a great desire to explore—new things, new opportunities—and to garner a few new skill sets. As I sought to emancipate myself financially, I was dead set on not passing up any job opportunity.

I combed through newspapers for many hours regularly—meticulously, slowly sifting through them, searching, reading everything and everywhere. Success would conclude my quest. At times I felt as though I needed more eyes. I read every possible poster with job offerings. I was like a tracker dog locked on a scent—my independence was out there, and there was no eluding me.

I got news one day—I can't quite recall from whom—our local jerk center was hiring workers, but only for the summer.

I felt an oven in my chest. My heart warmed. My eyes watered. I thought: *Yes, my big opportunity!* Everyone loved the restaurant that specialized in jerk pork and chicken—Jamaican specialties—and had a bar also.

It was as if, for weeks, I'd been lost at sea. Now, finally, land—just a little over the horizon. Inquiring within the establishment, I was invited to apply directly to the owner.

I had not the slightest idea how to write a job application. I hadn't written one before. The last few years of high school would have really made a difference—needless to say. I would not let that deter me from applying and claiming financial freedom.

Desperation begets results at times. I somehow managed to conjure up an application, place it into an envelope, and seal it.

To ensure that my application reached him, I walked to the business owner's home for a hand delivery. I thought it was best I deliver it myself. He knew my parents well, and I thought he might not be offended if I turned up at his gates.

He lived about two miles from my house on a long, asphalted, yet dusty road. As I walked to his house, the sun beamed down on me; I felt as though I was in an oven. Rays of heat rose from the earth like steam from a pot of boiling water.

Perspiration flowed from my face—my lips were now dry and parched. It was as if my saliva had somehow evaporated, leaving my throat itchy. But I was so consumed by my mission I had forgotten to take water on my journey. It was crucial I get this job, and I went after it.

I was relieved to have somehow managed to arrive at the gate of the business owner. I paused to catch my breath; peering over, I noticed his parked pick-up truck on his drive.

At that moment, I reassured myself—he was home. I knocked and waited with bated breath for a positive response. A member of his family answered, and I asked whether he was at home. They told me to wait; he would soon attend to me.

I waited patiently—not as though I had an option, even though the wait seemed like an eternity.

I was determined not to be put off by it but to give myself a fair chance. I believe when you want something badly enough, you will stop at nothing.

I wanted that job badly. I had a child to feed, and the doors to the only place I was sure to receive food were shut for the next eight weeks. I was not willing to battle with hunger during this period.

The owner came to the gate, and I explained that I was looking for a job. He noticed the desperation on my sun-drenched, sweat-dripping face. I quivered as I reached for the envelope deep down in my skirt pocket. It felt as though it had been kept in the dew. My hands quivered with fear as I handed it over. He read my application and told me to come with him to his establishment. He appeared dressed for the office.

I hopped into his pickup truck and took my seat behind him. He reversed the truck slowly, then sped down the road.

I didn't even think about not taking a ride from a stranger. As I look back, he wasn't really a stranger, though. He was known as the wealthy business owner whose business brought jobs and life to the community.

As we continued in the pick-up, we soon arrived at the jerk center. It must have taken less than twenty minutes. I had no watch, no mobile phone, or any form of portable timepiece back then.

He took me to his office and gave me a math test, asked a few questions—I suppose we could call it an interview—and told me I would hear from him soon. Feeling really positive, I left.

The jerk center was strategically placed near a road junction where two other thriving businesses were located—a construction and a beverage company. It was a very popular entertainment spot—attracting rum drinkers, jerk pork and jerk chicken eaters, and partygoers. It had the feel and setting of a holidaymaker's spot. The bar was situated under a gazebo close to the front of the premises, with the open-plan kitchen adjacent to it.

From about half a mile from the center, you could smell the tantalizing aroma of marinated jerk meat being cooked. The famous ingredients in the jerk recipe include pimento, scotch bonnet pepper, spring onion, thyme, and other spices. Blended together, the spices give a distinct aroma that cannot be mistaken. You'd know the aroma wafted to your nostrils from the jerk center kitchen, carried off by the wind, making the whole area fragrant. The aroma stimulates our nostrils and taste buds, causing us to salivate even if we are not lovers of meat.

A few days after I sat for the test and interview, I received the wonderful news: "I'm happy to tell you you've passed, and you are hired!"

Woohoo, what great news!

I firmly believe determination is the key to success. Determination landed me my first job—bartending! My role included serving alcoholic beverages, pork menus, and cigarettes—among other items you would usually find in a bar.

Although I was not going to church and practicing my faith anymore, I still believed in the teachings of the Bible. A well-known verse says, *Train up a child in the way he should go, and when he is old, he will not depart from it (Proverbs 22:6 KJV).* I departed from the church but never from the Lord. In retrospect, I realized that hunger and desperation forced me into a position outside my morals—outside what society would expect of me as a Christian.

But I had to make a conscious decision. Even though those thoughts were at the back of my mind, my only instinct was to survive. Destitution was not an option for me anymore. I was not willing to bargain with hunger and suffering at that moment.

Even though I was in a place I wasn't supposed to be—that is, serving in a bar—I believed myself fortunate. It meant I was able to buy milk, soap, and nappies for my baby.

Under normal circumstances, if I were to walk into a bar to purchase alcohol and cigarettes, they would not have been sold to me, given I was a minor. However, I felt I had been favored with this job. My flour and oil were certain for the duration of that employment.

It reminds me of a Bible story from Luke 15:11-32. In the story, a man had two sons. The younger asked his dad for his portion of the inheritance, which was not even due—not till after the death of his parents. But it was given to him, and he went on a long journey to a faraway land, where he wasted it on wild living.

After he wasted all his fortune, a severe famine hit the country; the son found himself in dire situations—I guess like mine. He took a job feeding pigs—in due course, growing so destitute that he even longed to eat the food allotted to the pigs.

Eventually, the young man came to his senses and remembered his father. In humility, he recognized his foolish behavior and decided to return to his birthland and ask for forgiveness and mercy. His father, who had been watching and waiting, received him back with open arms of love and compassion. In fact, he was delighted by the return of his lost son.

Likewise, I knew I should not be working in a bar; I was living a life not pleasing to God. I desired to return too, but I was not strong enough to make that decision at that time. I told myself, "One day, God's gonna work something out, so I return to him fully. Our Father in Heaven loves lost sinners, and his love brings them back to the right relationship with Him."

Day one on the job was exciting. I turned up at work on time and ready for the tasks that lay ahead. Not knowing what to expect, I was understandably nervous.

In order to learn the art of bartending, I was invited to shadow the other workers. I worked with enthusiasm and diligence, acquiring the skill quite quickly. The owner was pleased with my performance, and it was not long before I started running my own shift. I made friends with the customers and learned about their preferences so I could personalize their service.

I learned the names of as many customers as I could. So, when addressing them, I used their titles and last names as a mark of respect and connection. Culturally, to call an adult by their first name is deemed disrespectful.

Given my age of sixteen-plus years at that time, almost every person who stepped onto the premises was older than I, although no one knew my age. Not even the manager—he did not ask. I presumed that because I had a child, he assumed I was an adult.

Remembering the patrons' names let them feel valued, and they kept coming. Also, I learnt about their favorite drink and special menus. So, the next time they returned to the bar, I would say something like, "Nice to see you today, Mr. Brown. How are you? Are you having a gin and tonic? Is that with a pound of jerk?" There were times when they told me to let them have the same thing. Meaning their usual order. So, it was important to know what that was.

Several patrons liked my customer service and kept coming back. This increased my sales. My boss was happy. My experience grew quickly, and so did the number of customers who came out on the nights I worked.

My sales figure averaged and sometimes exceeded that of the more experienced workers. Little did I know that I had exceeded the manager's expectations. As a result, I was retained on staff after the probationary period.

I continued the job for several months beyond TMP's reopening for the new term and beyond my seventeenth birthday. I felt a level of independence because I was able to care for myself and my son without being overly dependent on anyone or TMP.

I went to the project during weekdays, working at the jerk center in the evenings. This, while being a full-time single parent, was a difficult balance. But I was determined to push ahead to make something positive of my life and build a brighter future for my son, whom I loved with all my heart.

Watching my son grow was an inspiration. I was now able to buy him little things, such as clothing and small, inexpensive toys. Everyone called him my handbag. We went everywhere together, except work. He was like a permanent fixture on my hip, the place I carried him. I did not have a stroller or baby carriage. I loved when he was on my hip, as I could fully support him in that position.

My son's name is Andre, and his nickname is Bugz. In my eyes, he was the cutest baby ever to grace planet Earth. Unfortunately, not many people, if any, shared my views. He had large ears sticking off his head like a bunny rabbit's and a slightly disfigured forehead, which was caused by my ignorance.

Upon Andre's birth at the hospital, the nurse washed and dressed him, handing him to me before placing him in the bassinet at my bedside. I took a deep look at him, and frankly, I didn't like how his head was shaped—like a cone.

I began imagining him going to school and being jeered at or bullied. Hence, I set about to reshape his head with my hands! His head was soft, like freshly laid eggs. I felt I could make it round before it got hard.

I recalled my mother raised hens, and we usually picked up eggs from around the yard where the hens laid them. If we did not take them up quickly, other animals ate or destroyed them. We knew when the hen was about to lay, and we would grab them just as they were laid. However, sometimes, an egg had not yet hardened and broke.

I thought it was the same with the baby's head, so I wanted to quickly reshape it before it hardened! Oh, my days! How ignorant I was.

I began gently pressing on one side of Andre's forehead with my cuffed palm, trying to make his head round. Just then, the midwife saw and shouted at me to stop. Saved by the bell! I sighed later.

On reflection, I thank God for the nurse shouting at me. I must say, I am disgusted with anyone who shouts at another person, especially when it's a professional. However, this is the one shouting I've appreciated. I do not want to imagine what would have happened had the midwife not seen what I was doing and stopped me.

I could have caused serious brain damage and global developmental delay if not death.

Growing up, barbers struggled to line up Andre's hair front. Now that Andre is an adult, we were chit-chatting about life one day when he asked, "Mummy, why is my head shaped like this? Barbers find it hard to shape the front."

"Son, you don't want to know," I commented.

"Tell me, Mummy."

"Well, if you really want to know what happened . . . When you were born, you had a cone-like–shaped head. I didn't like it, and I tried to fix it myself."

"What you mean, fix it yourself?"

"I started to reshape your head with my hands, but the nurse saw and stopped me almost instantly."

"Muuum!" (emphasizing the u in "Mum"). "You're crazy?" he replied frighteneedly. "You could have killed me or damaged my brain!"

I saw how taken aback Andre was. But he gave that affectionate, cute smile that always reminds me of his paternal aunt, Marcia.

Thank God, nothing worse happened. Both of us laughed at my ignorance and, from time to time, joked about it.

But on a more serious note, I reflected that at Andre's birth, no family member was with me: no friends, no support, no guidance, no one holding my hands during delivery, no one rejoicing that a life had come into the world, and no one to counsel me on motherhood. Nevertheless, a young life was entrusted to my care, and I was doing what I thought was best at the time.

What is expected from a sixteen-year-old mum with little or no social support? Little did I know how God would use these experiences to prepare me for the job I'm now doing.

Let me assure you, with God, no experience is wasted.

It was while I was working at the jerk center, my liberation as I called it, that love came knocking at my heart's door again—so I thought.

I met Delroy, a respectable young man well-known in the community. He had an aura that shouted discipline, respect, and authority!

He was the undercover armed-security officer for the business. Not every patron knew his role. You could say he was the element of surprise for the would-be robbers. We became friends, enjoying spending time together.

There was something special about the way he talked with me. I felt safe. He showed sustained interest in my well-being, and he made it his responsibility to ensure I got home safely at night.

The community was notorious for gun crime, rape, robbery, and murder. My shifts finished at midnight, and most nights, I had to walk home. The main source of public transport was taxis. They were not frequent or available at that time of night.

I lived approximately two miles from the jerk center. My community was not well-lit. Lamp posts were long distances apart. As a matter of fact, my street had none. The only lights were dim glares from homes. My street—about half a mile long—was overgrown with tall, shady trees in some spots.

At night you could hold the darkness in your hands. I was very afraid to take that walk. Many nights, my heart almost pounded out of my chest at the slightest sound. Sometimes it was animals in the bushes and not people wanting to do harm, as I feared. Walking with someone I trusted kept anxiety from preying on me.

After many nights of sharing thoughts as Delroy walked home with me, I trusted him and had confidence in him. Hence, when he asked me to be his girlfriend, I happily succumbed. Because, as I've said, my life was like a ship on tempestuous seas, battered and torn. I thought he would be the captain to navigate it to shore.

I began imagining Delroy being that caring dad to Andre and a faithful provider. My stabilizer, my burden bearer, my poverty rescuer, my love and joy-giver. Did I say my husband forever?

Delroy was his mother's only child. I later found her to be a sweet, kind, and caring soul. One I took as a mother, who became my friend, defender, and confidant. Yes, that's truly Miss Etta. I thought I would make the perfect daughter-in-law and a welcome addition to the family.

Hand in hand, we strolled the long walk home down the stretch of a pitch-black, dark road with sparsely twinkle patches of a star-lit sky.

Whenever I arrived at my gate, goodbye became so hard to say with just one word. At times instead of bidding each other goodbye, we would stand at the gate where our shadows become one, and we'd talk for hours into the wee hours of the morning.

Many times, our conversation was promising and made me hopeful. It was never short of a compliment that often had me smiling to myself.

He was such a great listener that I could tell him anything and everything. It's the relationship I wished I'd had with my parents and siblings. His compassion and affection filled the long-existent void.

For a while, everything was just blissful. I was happy again. The Bible says *a merry heart does good, like medicine* (Proverbs 17:22 NKJV). This was truly my experience. My smiles were like the morning sun—bright and energy-giving. My newfound happiness put a spring into my step, giving new meaning to life. I felt I could conquer the world!

My friends and the staff at TMP noticed and wanted to know the reason I was glowing. My friends felt I was favored by some staff and that I might be receiving extra privileges. However, that was not so. I told my trusted friends that I had met someone but not to tell the staff.

In retrospect, I learnt that sometimes being too open about your personal life can make you vulnerable. I later discovered that one of my best friends was jealous of my happiness and wanted to destroy me. Oblivious to that, I became easy prey.

As young, vulnerable, inexperienced mothers and mothers-to-be, we yearned for stability. The reality was only a few TMP participants were still in relationships with their child's father. From our conversations, I knew it was our desire to form stable relationships. We wanted a healthy family life—we were all from broken, dysfunctional, or chaotic homes.

In hindsight, I realized that my best friend envied me—what appeared to be a blissful relationship. I often shared some intimate moments, not realizing the depth of her jealousy until I learnt that she had betrayed me by exposing what I thought was a well-hidden secret. But hey-ho! It was all part of my process—leading to where God wanted me to be.

Let me quickly say my season of happiness with Delroy was short-lived—a euphoric moment—but had lifetime consequences. Clearly, I hadn't learnt from my first mistake.

At age seventeen-plus, I again became pregnant. Was it a mistake? You decide. They say you never make the same mistake twice. The second time you make it, it is no longer a mistake. It is a choice.

Looking back, becoming pregnant might have been my subconscious choice. I say this because I knew very well that I could become pregnant if I had unprotected sex. But—Oops! I did it again!

By now, I'd stopped working, which meant my situation had moved to a higher level of consequence.

I thought: *If ever I needed God, it's now!*

As I've said before, TMP was for first-time mothers and mothers-to-be only. A second pregnancy meant I had violated the conditions of placement at the center. Without an income or a strong support network, it was going to be a tough road ahead.

Delroy realized the enormity of my problem and tried to take remedial actions, or so he thought. He reasoned: Being so young—eighteen—a mother of two children, with very little help from anyone, would push me over the edge.

Moreover, we thought that neither of our parents would be happy. Our relationship was just developing; we hadn't even introduced each other to our families properly. Very few people knew we were seeing each other.

Delroy felt hugely responsible because he was older than I, and we had agreed not to have an unplanned pregnancy. One evening we were discussing the pregnancy and plans for moving forward. Delroy said to me, "Why don't you have an abortion?"

"Abortion?" I responded. *You mean I should kill my baby?* A question on the tip of my lips but never uttered.

"Yes, Marva, you need to have an abortion. We can't afford another baby."

Mur-derrr! Mur-derrr! Mur-derrr!—rang out in my head like the chiming bells in the ancient Presbyterian Church on Sunday mornings.

Immediately, I remembered similar advice my doctor had given me when he found out I was pregnant previously. Although I did not want to be pregnant again, I did not want a termination either.

"You have to have an abortion," he pressed.

I felt I was being forced to terminate the pregnancy, but I was afraid to speak out further. Not that Delroy would hurt me or anything like that, but I just didn't have the courage to say anything else. Boldness hadn't gotten hold of me yet.

The conversation was punctuated with long pauses and silences as we listened to our thoughts—or was it God speaking?

In the late 1980s, around the time of my pregnancy, abortion was illegal in Jamaica. It still is today—except in extenuating circumstances. However, it is well known that abortion is quite popular, and medical experts perform it.

Women who are poor and have an unwanted pregnancy rely on traditional remedies or 'botched specialists,' as they cannot afford the private cost to have it done properly.

Abortion is a taboo topic; women are shunned for having it. The situation was made worse by Dancehall lyrics, and the songs were aired on public broadcasting networks.

In Patois, the phrase for abortion is "dash weh belly" (throw away belly).

Delroy and I continued to speak in a silent tone for a prolonged period before I broke the silence with a calm, soft tone.

"I cannot have an abortion here (at home). If anyone finds out, it would be a worse embarrassment for me."

"You don't need to go to the doctor; there is a bush you can boil and drink, and your period will come back," he explained.

"Bush! What bush? What's the name of that bush?" I probed in disbelief.

"I don't know the name; it grows wild," he continued.

"Well, you will need to get it because I don't know it," I uttered with sarcasm, not hiding my resentment of the idea.

"It sells in Coronation Market, Downtown Kingston. I will get some on my way from work tomorrow."

He had a daytime job in that area and worked at the jerk center at night.

"OK, what did you say I should do with it again?"

"Boil it and drink it."

"It's better if you boil it at your house and bring it to me. I cannot do that here."

"No problem. I'll do it," he replied confidently.

The conversation paused, and silence took over. "The church bell began to chime in my head again, *Murderrr! Murderrr!* As the chimes grew louder and louder, it was evident that they could only be heard by me.

Simultaneously, a popular song echoed in my ears.

Walking cemetery, the gal a walking cemetery

Dash weh belly, the gal a dash weh belly

(In the dialect patois, Dash-weh means throw-away).

Was *Murder She Wrote* flashing before my closed eyes? I felt I was back in the emotional turmoil from less than two years ago.

Delroy, it was obvious to me, did not consider my feelings, particularly what an abortion would do to me emotionally.

Albeit I was resolute in my heart that I would not terminate my pregnancy, Delroy continued to talk about preparation for an abortion.

I knew the road ahead would be rough and tough. Nevertheless, I was willing to go on that journey.

I believed I would defy the odds. My first pregnancy was a mistake. Can I say the same for the second?

Consequently, my feelings towards Delroy changed. I did not feel in love anymore because instead of what I thought would be joy, my life was spiralling downhill into chaos.

Back at TMP, I did not tell my friends, or anyone for that matter. I carried on, participating fully.

My baby bump was very small—no one could tell what it was. Every day, I wore the same loose-fitting dress, as I did not have other choices; it hid the baby bump well. I always washed and ironed it every single day, ensuring I kept good hygiene and in no way called attention to myself.

The summer break came, and my half-sister, Lorna, took me to live with her family. She lived in an adjoining parish—far away from my house. I was happy to move to a new area. I felt I could make a fresh start after I had my baby.

Lorna, my half-sister, is our father's first child. She is tall—well over six feet. So was her love and compassion towards me—tall and immeasurable! I believed God sent her to rescue me from destitution. Hence, I did not struggle as much compared with my first pregnancy.

Lorna was like a mother, taking care of me and never judging or ridiculing me. She not only provided for my physical needs but also catered to my social and emotional development.

We bonded well, and I was happy living with her. I baby-sat my niece and nephew while she and her husband went to work. I did not have to worry about anything. Lorna was proactive, and she ensured my every need was taken care of. Thinking back, I feel indebted to my beloved sister Lorna.

After a few weeks in my new environment, I made friends with some of Lorna's friends, and my social network began to grow. They showed keen interest in my well-being, and everyone looked forward to the arrival of my baby.

On the due date, I delivered at the city hospital—unbeknownst to anyone at TMP. My sister and her friends supported me, and I felt happy and relaxed, unlike at the end of my first pregnancy, when I was scared and alone.

I named him Adrion, wanting his name to sound similar to Andre's. I imagined both growing up like twins. Adrion was tiny, weighing approximately four pounds at birth. He could be held easily in the palm of one of my hands.

I thanked God for a safe delivery. There were some worries we had to overcome initially. However, upon his birth, he had no health issues.

The most unexplainable emotion flooded my heart as I held him in my arms. I showered my love on him as I recalled the conversation with his dad about aborting him. I was overjoyed and thanked God I hadn't. If I had, I would have been left with nothing but bitter memories. His cute little face melted my heart.

I recall it says in the Bible, "*When a woman gives birth, she has a hard time; there's no getting around it. But when the baby is born, there is joy in the birth. This new life in the world wipes out memory of the pain*" (John 16:21, MSG).

This was truly my experience; the joy of seeing Adrion wiped away all the pain, hurt, and upset about becoming pregnant a second time. I was wondering: *Is he the same little boy who was kicking inside my tummy?* God is truly amazing.

I was discharged into my sister's care, along with my bundle of joy—to love and care for him, at least for the next eighteen years, I thought.

Delroy visited us at home. You could tell he was happy to see us, and he loved his son. He was very attentive, ensuring that Andre did not poke Adrion in his eyes or try to lift him on his lap.

Delroy fully embraced his new role as a father, including financially. We were no longer in a relationship, but we were amicable. He made arrangements for his mother and grandmother to meet their grandchild. He knew his mother would be happy because Adrion was her only grandson.

I continued to live at my sister's, so when Andre and I did not return to TMP after the summer break, TMP came looking for us. They checked at our former home and learned I was living with one of my sisters in another parish.

TMP pleaded for our return to the project and promised me access to additional help. Albeit, they did not know I had another baby. Therefore, Lorna reluctantly agreed I should return home, from where TMP was more accessible. She wanted me to take and pass my CXC (Caribbean Examination Council) exams so that I would have better education and job opportunities.

I took Adrion to his paternal grandmother, who was overjoyed to see him. She immediately fell in love with him and offered to babysit while I attended the program with Andre.

Everyone was happy I returned to the project and was hoping I would ace my exams. However, I dreaded TMP finding out I had a second child, as this would be a huge let-down.

In hindsight, when I was encouraged to return to the project, I should have been open and honest. However, I gave in to my fears and went down a path of deception to protect my pride.

I was tired of the grip hunger and poverty had on me. I wanted to break free.

One afternoon while at TMP, I was called to Mrs. Burrell's office. She was the center manager. Almost all the participants had left the compound. I popped into the office joyfully, believing it was one of those regular moments when one of the managers would send me to the market to purchase fresh food and vegetables—an errand I enjoyed.

One of the coordinators, Mrs. Joseph (not her correct name), especially liked my choice of yams, oranges, and pumpkins. She told me my choice of pumpkins made tasty soups. That made me feel valued because at least that one thing I was doing right.

I recalled the sobering evening when I stepped into Mrs. Burrell's office. I felt a heavy silence fall upon the room. It was like a naughty employee being called to a board room.

From my recollection, all the key management personnel were sitting, awaiting my entry. Alas, their faces told the story. They need not say a word—busted!

I walked slowly to the only empty seat left in the tightly cramped room. It appeared that the well-positioned seat was left vacant purposely for me. It was in the center of an arched row of seats, the chairs arranged in front of Mrs. Burrell's desk. Everyone could see my face clearly.

I sat with my head hanging down, staring at my lap and the area of flooring where my feet rested. I could not look into anyone's face because they were shouting silently:

"You are a cheat! You should not be here! You have ruined your chance to turn your life around! Foolish girl!"

My thoughts fleeted, and I shivered like a suffering infant on a cold cot. Then the answer came—you're caught!

Embarrassment and fear held me by my throat, snuffing my life out of my body. I anticipated what was to come. I knew that was a deciding moment and a turning point in my life.

Glancing across the flooring, I felt piercing eyes penetrating me. I wanted to scream, "Have mercy upon me!

I've now learnt my lesson. It will not happen again. Do not kick me out," but then I whispered in my own ears, "Silence is golden."

"Marva, you've had us on a long joy ride," a sharp voice interrupted the silence.

I didn't understand the phrase then, so I replied, "No, I've not."

"You certainly have," another voice responded.

"When were you going to tell us you had a second child?"

"Me, Miss? I do not have a second child!" I lied defiantly.

"Marva, didn't you have a second pregnancy?"

"Nope, I didn't!" My vehement denial continued.

"Where is Adrion?" one of the voices pressed.

Adrion? Where did they get that information? I pondered silently.

"Where is your boyfriend?" someone else asked.

The questions were coming in thick and fast—like bullets from a pistol.

"I do not have a boyfriend," I mumbled.

"Where is Adrion's father? How long have you been seeing each other? Has he been helping you?" were some of the questions being asked.

Looking back, it was like sitting in a witness box on trial for a heinous crime. I realized they had made their inquiries and were in possession of facts—full details of Adrion's birth.

Clearly, they must have spoken with the hospital. That's the only place where those details were held, I contemplated.

There was no point continuing to deny that Adrion existed. But I wasn't gonna add any more information than they already held; my survival depended on continuing to enroll at the center. There was no getting out of this, though.

I'm doomed!—at least, so I thought then.

In a partial dismissal from the project, I was only allowed to attend the classes that were preparing me for the CXC exams. These were held on the outside of the building that housed the program.

It was made clear that the program was for first-time mothers only. I felt disappointed in myself; I'd let down everyone again. However, I thank TMP for allowing me to sit for my exams.

Unfortunately, I was not allowed in the building except to use the restrooms. I was not allowed to converse with other participants in the program, not even with those I'd formed close friendships with.

By now, you don't need me to tell you it was a devastating blow—crushing for me on all levels.

My friends at the project were my support network. Being cut off from them meant I was socially isolated.

The project stopped supplying me with food and bus fare, which meant my problems increased, and so did the days of hunger!

I felt further rejected and bewildered—shipwrecked!

I continually had thoughts I was a failure and that I was no good.

These thoughts occupied most of my waking moments, but deep down in my heart, I resolved to make good of my life—defy the odds and prove everyone, including the statistics about teenage pregnant mums, wrong!

Despite the harsh sanction by TMP, I still felt a deep sense of gratitude for the love and support they had shown previously—which helped me develop a strong mindset and great inner strength.

I remember TMP held a program known as the *Big Sister Club*. This was a group-counseling session where the mothers and mothers-to-be met in a small group with one of the teachers (*a big sister*). The *big sister* in my group was Mrs. Burrell. In the session, we could open up with the support of our *big sister* and also share with others. These moments were invaluable.

Mrs. Burrell was straight-talking and did not let her power and authority get in the way of meeting us at our level. She was empathic and highly attuned to our needs—commanding our respect. When our circumstances weighed us down or even knocked us over, she knew how to pick us up.

In retrospect, Mrs. Burrell was the woman for the job—the epitome of motherhood, kindness, and love.

I remember Mrs. Burrell extending herself to help my mother in a medical emergency. She transported Mama in her private car to the doctor—ensuring she was looked after. I must let you know that when distressed, Mama wasn't the nicest of patients. So, you can imagine what happened that day when Mrs. Burrell became her ambulance driver and attending nurse. Thank you, Mrs. Burrell. TMP was a holistic support for me—truly a lifeline.

The discipline doled out to me meant I lost this vital support. Nevertheless, I held fast to the training I'd garnered. Moving on, during my darker days, I took encouragement from those pep talks that told me: "Teenage pregnancy is not the end of your journey; you can turn your life around. You can become anything you want to be."

As drilled into our thoughts and being by Mrs. Burrell, I believed it, fully accepted it, and made peace with myself, knowing I had messed up—again. No one was to be blamed but me.

In hindsight, I'm truly grateful that TMP allowed my first son, Andre, to continue in the project for children, which gave him an excellent start to his early years. At that crucial stage, he was shaped by his experiences, completely dependent on me to facilitate them. Therefore, my actions had a defining impact on enabling him to reach his full potential. This kind of start, I could not have given him without the tremendous support of TMP.

During those times, I constantly worried about my situation. Although I attended classes, it was challenging to concentrate on what was being taught. I was present in body but absent in mind.

I lacked focus and motivation, and I dreaded being labeled a failure. I wanted to put my priorities right, although the odds were against me.

I was ashamed and disgusted with myself. However, I believed success to be still attainable, and the only way to achieve it was to make the decision to go after it.

The time came, and our small class of four mothers took the final exams in May–June. The results came later, and in September of that same year, the project sent three mothers to a teacher training college. Because of my second pregnancy, I was the only mother from the class who did not receive a tertiary educational placement.

I guess you can just imagine how broken, devastated, and rejected I felt. I reflected on my situation and accepted it for what it was. But why should they send me to college, anyway? The program was for first-time mothers only. Nevertheless, giving up was not an option. I was determined to defy the odds.

Often when my mother is faced with challenges, she repeats the popular phrase, *"When the going gets tough, the tough get going."* I adopted that phrase as my go-to self-motivational phrase.

I did not give up on myself, and instead of ending up a reject, God empowered me through my adversities and turned my life around.

One night as I walked through my rugged, rough, dark dirt road to get home, I met Mervin, a man well respected in the community. Though it was dark, he saw how I tightly held my sons in my arms as I hurried home. He stopped me and, with a deep sense of care and compassion, spoke to me about getting my life back on track. He did not ridicule me, as did my older siblings.

He told me how I could become either a police officer, teacher, or nurse, despite having no money and poor grades. That pep talk changed the trajectory of my life. I immediately decided to join the police force. It was a light bulb moment! Sparks went off in my heart and head—the light at the end of a long, dark tunnel.

The following day I journeyed to Kingston—the country's capital. I had no money except my bus fare. I did not know how long the exam would take—whether I would need to be at the center all day or just a few hours. My focus was on taking the first step—getting to the center and passing the entrance exam.

While I was traveling to the center, I started visualizing myself as a police officer. I saw myself in uniform, patrolling in squad cars with lights flashing, maintaining law and order, protecting and improving the quality of life for people. The prospect excited me. I was motivated and determined. Nothing would stop me from achieving my dream of becoming the civil servant I so wanted to become.

I did not have money—not even to buy a sweet. I had not taken any food with me, either. I had not thought of lunch because it was a rare meal for me. Not because I was on any diet restriction but simply because I could not afford to eat three meals a day.

Eventually, with a mix of excitement and anxiety, I arrived at the location. I completed the preliminaries, and a police officer directed me to a large classroom-like examination room.

As I walked in, the desks and chairs stared me in the face, reminding me that I was a high-school dropout, a teen mother, a single parent of two children, who had disappointed her family, community, and peers.

The school furniture brought back to mind that, in the final exams earlier that year, their counterparts had witnessed my poor performance. Nevertheless, I looked intensely at them and silently took my seat in the middle of the room. I was determined to redeem my earlier performance.

Candidates of police-like stature and presentation quickly filled the room, which ended my conversation with those inanimate objects. I became uneasy, fearing I might not pass. So, I encouraged myself to press forward, think positively, and banish thoughts of defeat.

Carefully, parceling out the allotted time, I worked through the questions. Afterwards, the examiners placed us in two groups—successful and unsuccessful. They did not say which was which. However, in one group, over three-quarters of the candidates lined up. I was in the smaller group; terrified, I silently prayed that I had passed. I felt I did well, but given my chain of disappointments, my confidence was sapped. I started normalizing disappointment. However, to the disappointment of the larger group, they were the ones sent away.

I felt on a high because I had tasted success at last. The police officers congratulated us, announcing that that same afternoon we would move to stage two. They told us we should have our lunch and resume at the time they gave us. It was only then that I realized my dilemma—I had no food or money, and the examination stages would last until the end of the day.

As the minutes passed in silent reflection, my tummy rumbled, and my mouth secreted whitish mucus at both corners. I licked my lips continuously, but my saliva was too dry to moisten it. I felt I had no other option but to use the money for my return bus fare to buy food and ease the hunger pangs. I was determined to complete what I'd started.

Finally, the day ended, and I succeeded in all stages and was given a date for an interview. I felt thrilled and empowered, starting to see daylight at the end of my tunnel.

I went to the bus station to travel back home, and it was now dark. There lurked a man of seemingly evil intentions, trying to persuade me to follow him down a street that was well-known for crimes of all sorts.

"Young girl are you going to May Pen?" he asked.

I bowed my head in acknowledgement—fearfully.

"Let me show you where the buses are parked. Come with me," he instructed. "You won't get any bus here at this time. They park at a different spot in the evenings. Come on, come let me show you the May Pen buses."

I knew he was lying. I was aware that the buses parked outside the designated bus park after business hours. And I also knew that the location I was in was where the buses stopped. I realized this man was trying to trap me, and I was scared and afraid, even though a small crowd of passengers gathered, waiting on buses too.

It appeared he knew—because I was hesitant to get into previous buses, and I looked worried—I had no bus fare. After that encounter, I got into the next bus that came. It was one of those large-capacity minibuses. I stood on the steps to let fare-paying passengers be seated.

Fear gripped me. Not because I was dangerously hanging on the bus steps as it sped along but because I had no money and anticipated another embarrassing moment. I traveled standing until there were few empty seats.

As we were about halfway through our journey, the bus conductor shouted, "All fares, please!" As he looked in my direction, my heart pounded, and my pulse raced. "I am the sister of" (I gave my eldest brother's name). He was popular, and chances were, the conductor might know him.

My brother was like the main family breadwinner. A mechanic, he operated a garage and a taxi. In fact, he was the only sibling with sustained income. The rest of us, including my mother, were just getting by. But he had his own home and a family. Most of us depended on him for financial aid. Perhaps not surprisingly, I guess he had become weary of always doling out funds, which made it very difficult for any of us to get a penny from his pocket.

The conductor looked at me again.

"I have no fare," I uttered timidly. My brother will pay. He's at home."

The conductor's jaw dropped, and eyes widened. He uttered not a word. Neither did any of the passengers, but I interpreted their silence while hoping my brother was really at home.

On approaching my brother's house, I asked the driver to stop at his gate, then ran to the back of the house, where he was working. "Brother! Brother!" I explained frantically. "I took the police test, and I passed. I'm coming from Kingston, and I have no fare; see, the bus is waiting . . ." I pleaded my case.

He looked at me disdainfully as if to say, "It's not possible you passed." I looked at him again and repeated my plea.

"Brother, please help me; I need bus fare."

In the meantime, the driver kept tooting the horn as if to say, "Where are you? Hurry up. Bring my fare!"

My brother did not believe I had passed the test but eventually pulled the coins from his pocket. I sighed a great relief, thanking God he was home.

I reflected that had I not gotten into that bus at the time I did, my story would probably be different. I sensed that the man at the bus stop wanted to rape me.

God was surely with me—I triumphed over what was a difficult situation. I could have been a crime statistic.

The late famous soul singer Sam Cooke once sang about living being hard, but he was scared of dying.

The chorus reads:

It's been a long, a long time comin',

But I know a change gon' come, oh yes, it will[1]

I counseled myself that change would come only when I behaved differently. I encouraged myself in the Lord. I trusted in His power to change my situation, not letting my circumstances keep me down. I forgave myself and moved on.

There was no space in my mind and no time to wallow in self-pity. I had to learn, and I learned fast. I acknowledged my situation as it was—a two-time teen mum and a high-school drop-out—but my life still lay ahead of me.

---

1 https://genius.com/Sam-cooke-a-change-is-gonna-come-lyrics

I had a mind makeover, telling myself I must stop engaging in self-defeating behavior, which was doing me no good and getting me nowhere. So, I decided to restrict my love life—no more boyfriends until I was mature enough to handle relationship issues.

Furthermore, being a Bible-believing young woman, I was convinced that my behavior did not please God. I recalled in the Big Sister Club at TMP, Mrs. Burrell, the Center manager, counseled us: "Sex is beautiful, a wonderful thing, but it is not for you; it's for married couples! If you girls are not careful, you will end up having baby after baby by different fathers. Is that the life you want for you and your child?"

These words were etched on my mind as an artist works on metal: a reminder that sex outside marriage was, biblically speaking, morally wrong. The Bible teaches that sex should take place only between a man and a woman in the confines of marriage. Therefore, I reasoned, I had no business doing what I did to end up with two babies at eighteen. Don't be fooled—I loved them like a world without end! They became my strength and joy.

As I reflect on my journey, this well-known verse acts as my mantra: "*Now all glory to God, who is able, through his mighty power at work within us, to accomplish infinitely more than we might ask or think*" (Ephesians 3:20 NLT).

In my spirit, I felt God was turning my life around, and change was on the way. This belief comforted me, motivated me, and kept me hopeful.

Sex and relationship education were crucial topics I still had much to learn about. I realized I was too young for motherhood. I was not mentally, emotionally, financially, or educationally prepared for child-rearing. Frankly, I had no business engaging in sex at my age then. Now, I've come to understand better that sex outside the confines of marriage is displeasing to God. There are consequences for our actions.

The Women's Bible, NJKV puts it this way:

Marriage is the second of two ancient, divine covenants bequeathed to the human family by our Creator (the Sabbath being the first). The inspired Word testifies that "marriage is to be held in honor among all, and the marriage bed is to be undefiled; for fornicators and adulterers, God will judge" (Hebrews 13:4). Two biblical books used the word "covenant" in describing this union between a man and a woman (Proverbs 2:17, Malachi 2:14). In fact, whether matrimony was arranged or included some kind of exchange or compensation, all unions were regarded as a covenant entered by the two families, signifying that it was, at once, a personal and a communal affair. In the beginning, when God created this covenant of love, there was no lavish ceremony of the type with which we are familiar. Back then, written manuals or established forms for the ceremony that pronounced a couple "husband and wife" did not exist. In fact, wedding rituals we hold sacred today began out of necessity and often self-preservation; they were handed down over the centuries and became important aspects of these ceremonies. The most important data about this sanctified relationship, this second covenant of love, can be found in Genesis 2:7, the very act of the creation story. We understand its origins, value, and permanency because it was introduced by God in Eden.

Takeaways

1. Turn your adversity into opportunity

I can assure you that life will not always be beautiful. Disappointment comes on us; hardship comes; events occur that bring us into difficult places. But remember not to pity yourself and give way to hopelessness. Discipline yourself to put in the effort to overcome distractions and harmful behaviors. Having an aim, a purpose, in life is key. Strengthen your mind by keeping focus, by sticking to the point as a compass to a pole.

The motivational writer Dr. Roopleen is credited with the following saying: "*Everything becomes attainable when you make up your mind to tap into your full potential, look for the positives in adverse situations, and turn adversity into opportunity. That's when you tip the odds in your favor.*"

2. Bouncing back

Love your child regardless of his/her mistakes. Love makes up for practically anything. If the child suffers adversity of any kind, if they feel loved by their parent or caregiver, the child has a higher probability of bouncing back.

3. A must-have

I must add that supportive networks are vital to overcoming adversities. I triumphed because, at crucial stages, people invested their time and resources to help me navigate those difficult situations. Good social support networks can help you through the stress of hard times. A lack of supportive networks can lead to isolation and loneliness.

4. Cry out to God

Just as a hungry child would call upon their parents, God allows trials to come upon us so that we may realize our inability to help ourselves and learn to call on Him for help. I am convinced that I overcame these difficult experiences because I cried out to the Lord in prayer, and He heard and answered me, even though I had backslidden. God loves sinners but not the sin!

Chapter 3
Baptism by Fire

You may be the only person left who believes in you, but it's enough. It takes just one star to pierce a universe of darkness. Never give up.

—Richelle E. Goodrich

After being successful in the police entrance exam, I waited anxiously for the interview date. I counted down daily, literally. I was eager to appease the many people I felt I had disappointed. Although I was neglected for a protracted time and my needs were never prioritized, still, I had this desire.

I tried not to torture my spirit by listening to toxic messages. It was important I stayed positive. I was determined to soar above my circumstances.

Then it finally arrived—the day I yearned for. I approached the gate of the police academy. Glancing around, I saw a long, steep, narrow, winding road awaiting me—definitely not what I had anticipated.

I started rationalizing my position to myself: This is where the police training takes place; the campus layout must have been designed purposely—fitness training begins with the first step inside!

The security personnel checked me over and instructed me to proceed to the administrative building. I footed it briskly up the hill while rehearsing some possible interview questions and answers.

As my eyes scanned the grounds to see if there were cameras affixed, I thought it was possible that people were being observed entering the compound. I was gasping halfway through my climb; it was as if somehow my breath had deserted me, but I still hurried. *Is someone sitting in a back office observing my agility?* I pondered. *Hopefully, that's not the case,* I reassured myself. *If so, they're certainly not impressed. And my prospect of becoming a police constable might be bleak.* Many weird thoughts crammed into my mind.

Never before had I received a formal interview, so this was my baptism by fire. To say I felt woefully unprepared was truly an understatement. I'd had zero material to study. Unlike CXC examinations, for which we prepare for two years by way of a syllabus and having access to past papers, this interview was the opposite. I knew that my success depended on preparation, yet I knew absolutely nothing about policing. I'd had no idea about the areas around which the questions would be based, and I made no inquiry.

As I plodded up the hill, I mulled over how I would present myself and whether I would satisfy the interviewer's criteria.

Nevertheless, I trekked across a huge open space. I would later discover its name to be "Parade Square," the location for graduation and other ceremonies.

As I began glimpsing the administrative building, my heart pounded faster and faster. It was as if a fist were inside my chest, speed-thumping its way to freedom. Anxiety grabbed me like it would a criminal trying to make a run for it. Though it was impossible, really, I tried my best to conceal my nervousness.

I started some positive self-talk: *You're worth it. You can do it. The interview will be just fine. You aced the entry exam you hadn't prepared for, and you will ace this interview too. You need to finish what you've started. You won't know if you will succeed unless you try. To quit is not an option*.

I felt my anxiety calming down gradually. I knew positive thinking was an effective way to manage stress as it improves our performance and general well-being. Furthermore, research—for example, at the Mayo Clinic—suggests that people with positive self-talk may have a host of health benefits, including "better coping skills during hardships and times of stress."[2] That is, mental skills that allow them to solve problems, think differently, and be more efficient at coping with challenges.[3]

Upon reaching the building, I realized there was an orderly queue waiting patiently to get inside. I was invited to join and took my position behind the last person in line. I counted around ten people immediately ahead of me, with others already in the building. How many were they hiring?

---

2 Walden University, "How Positive Self-Talk Can Make You Feel Better and Be More Productive," https://www.waldenu.edu/online-bachelors-programs/bs-in-psychology/resource/how-positive-self-talk-can-make-you-feel-better-and-be-more-productive#:~:text=Seeing%20Results,the%20positive%20may%20lead%20to%3A&text=Increased%20life%20span,Lower%20rates%20of%20depression .

3 Mayo Clinic Staff, "Positive Thinking" Stop Negative Self-Talk to Reduce Stress," https://www.mayoclinic.org/healthy-lifestyle/stress-management/in-depth/positive-thinking/art-20043950 .

They were admitting only a small number into the waiting area at a time. Once registered, I sat listening for them to call my name.

Almost everyone had sheets of paper, reading. I learnt later that they were studying questions and answers likely to be asked in the interview. Some were repeat candidates—interviewed previously but unsuccessful. I began thinking that if unsuccessful, I would not be the first or the last to fail the interview. I found peace in thinking of famous persons who were unsuccessful at an event but later succeeded. However, I quickly dismissed the thought of failing from my mind.

I was called to the waiting area inside the building. It was the office of the superintendent in charge of administration. I tried to distract myself by reading all the articles on display around the room. My eyes became fixed on the portraits of decorated officers arrayed neatly on the wall—officers who had served the police academy and retired.

They were all clad in uniform, including a cap and accoutrements. Looking dignified, depicting power and authority. Also, bellowing trust and honesty—I believe clothing makes a great first impression, and the police uniform is no different. Again, I saw myself dressed in a police uniform, maintaining an appearance of strength, safety, and security without instilling fear or intimidation.

My eyes turned to other information on the wall, but just then, I heard, “Miss Cunningham, will you come this way for us, please?”

I sprang to my feet and hurried into the office, where two men were sitting at a big, polished cedar desk. The

Jamaican flag stood in one corner of the very spacious, apparently hygienically well-maintained room.

Beginning with an initial bit of chitchat, evidently aimed at making me relax. Little did I know what was coming next.

The interview began, and the questions came, searchingly, piercing. Within a few minutes, it was obvious I was woefully unprepared. The officers were evidently resolute in their quest for the best candidates. And much to my disappointment, I was bowled over like a googly in a game of cricket in the scorching summer sun.

Several questions involved political affairs, locally and internationally. These areas were certainly not my strength. I had no interest in political matters. My innocent and immature view, then, was that political matters were for miserable, aged folks who had nothing else to do but complain about what the ruling party was doing wrong.

I was asked questions like: "Name three female prime ministers in the world."

I knew of Prime Minister Margaret Thatcher. *But who else was there?* I asked myself.

"Who is the Minister of National Security for Jamaica?"

My thought was: *Who cares who that minister is when my community is riddled with gun crime*?

"Who is the Youth and Culture Minister?"

Really, is there such a minister? So, why are there so many youths on my street without jobs, some not in school, and some having nothing to do?

My word! How unprepared, uninterested, and naïve I was! Yet, I was aiming to be a part of a law-enforcement body.

On the other hand, Jamaica has a history of protracted political conflict, often exploding in unrest that ripples across the country. For many years national and local elections were marred by violence, which impacted poor urban and rural communities greatly. My community was one such area. We were raised not to wear certain colors or sing certain songs publicly because they were aligned with a political party. And we could be targeted for exhibiting political allegiances. These and other factors contributed to my disinterest in anything to do with politics.

At the end of the interview, the officers told me promptly that I was unsuccessful; however, they could reinterview me in six weeks. I was comforted by the offer of a second interview; nevertheless, I felt deeply crushed, and my tears were welling up. I hurried out of the office so I could hide my watery eyes. As I passed several candidates outside, waiting to be interviewed, I tried to disguise my emotion.

I left the building and started making my way towards the main gate when disappointment gripped me, and I felt all the strength leave my legs. My knees weakened, making them incapable of carrying me any farther. I sat on a large rock underneath a huge shade tree, about one hundred and fifty yards from the administrative building. My eye muscles gave up, and an avalanche of tears flowed down my cheeks, dripping onto my shoulders and chest region, penetrating my blouse.

Even if Bob Marley stood beside me, whispering the lines from his "No Woman No Cry," trying to comfort me not to cry, tears would still flow—I would still be that woman crying.

One by one, candidates passed me by. Some appeared happy and joyful; others with long faces, crushed as I was.

After about twenty minutes, one of the interviewees stopped and asked if I was OK. I told him I performed poorly in the interview, so I was unsuccessful.

"Not to worry," he commented. "This is my second interview. I failed the first time, just like you. I felt disappointed too. But I went home and studied really hard, came back, and now I passed. You can do it too. Trust me. You will do better next time," he said reassuringly. "Here is a list of all the cabinet ministers and other information you need to know. Study it and prepare well for the next time. You have six weeks."

We continued to chat about general things for a short while; then, he wished me luck, bid me goodbye, and walked away slowly.

I felt a sense of calm come over me. I thought he must be an angel sent from above. I promised, no matter the situation, not to give up because God is able. *Failure teaches you that something can't be done—that way*—according to Thomas Edison, the masterful inventor of the telephone, the phonogram, and other inventions, all of which we take for granted today. *Never did he view mistakes as failures. They are simply opportunities to find out what doesn't work.*

In retrospect, before the interview, I should have made inquiries at the police department about how to prepare best; I didn't, much to my detriment. However, this was a learning curve—preparation is key to success. I promised myself to excel next time. I would pass the interview because I believe in the scriptures, which tell me I can do all things through Christ, who gives me strength (Philippians 4:13, New International Version).

With those thoughts in mind, I gathered my belongings, picked myself up, and continued my journey to the main gate, where I departed for home in a minibus.

On arriving, I did not tell anyone I failed the interview. I guess pride was setting in. I did not want to validate popular views about teen mums being failures. I wanted my siblings, and my mother especially, to celebrate something positive about me.

Moving forward, I devised a plan. It was to study daily, listen to the news, comb newspapers, and become more socially and politically aware—about not only national issues but internationally too.

It was now November. The participants at TMP had started their teacher training. I tried not to feel left behind, forgotten and ruined. I tried not to dwell on my mistakes; instead, I pressed on. Deep in the recesses of my heart, I felt God had a plan for me.

I did not believe the conversation I had that night with the man who told me about the police recruitment was coincidental. I'm convinced he was on a divine appointment to redirect me. He probably didn't even know it.

After we spoke, a sense of peace and calmness came over me. I realized that's how the Lord reassures me—I feel peace about a decision.

I used to call it my sixth sense, but I now know it's God speaking to me.

Six weeks elapsed from the date of my first interview. It was now time for the second. I felt prepared and confident. Nothing was going to get in my way to grasp this opportunity.

Benjamin Disraeli, nineteenth-century British prime minister, reportedly said, "The secret of success in life is for a man to be ready for his time when it comes."

This was my opportunity to become a policewoman. I had my second interview, and I smashed it, I might add!

I felt like I was riding high that day. I was overjoyed. The officers told me my background checks would be next. And if successful, I'd start training soon afterwards.

In the Bible, I see that the people God used to accomplish great things spent a lot of time preparing for what was a brief mission, which is an example for us. Determined to pass, I spent six weeks preparing for the interview. I did my part, fully confident that the Lord would do the rest.

This experience took me back to a story in the Bible—found in Matthew 9:20-22, Mark 5:25-34, and Luke 8:43-48. Jesus was healing, and a crowd of people gathered around. A woman in the crowd had endured nonstop bleeding for twelve years. Over the years, she had spent everything she had to pay doctors but with no improvement. In fact, she had gotten worse. She had heard about Jesus, so she pressed her way through the crowd and touched His robe. For she thought to herself: *If I can just touch His robe, I will be healed.* And so it was. The bleeding stopped immediately, and she could feel in her body that she had been healed of her terrible condition.

Jesus realized at once that healing power had gone out from Him, so he turned around in the crowd and asked, "Who touched my robe?"

His disciples answered, "Look at this crowd pressing around you. How can you ask, 'Who touched Me?'"

But he kept on looking around to see. Then the frightened woman, trembling at the realization of what had happened to her, came and fell to her knees in front of Him, admitting to Him what she had done. And He said to her, "Daughter, your faith has made you well. Go in peace. Your suffering is over" (Mark 5:25–34 NLT).

Takeaways

1. Be Intentional

In the story above, we saw that being intentional aided the woman in receiving her healing. Likewise, being intentional helped me pass the interview the second time around. I did not prepare for the first interview—I was not intentional. I thought that by just having a positive attitude, I would be able to give correct answers. However, this led to a rude awakening. I realized the necessity of being intentional, of putting in the work. That is, I then acquired the appropriate material and studied hard.

2. Have a Goal

Goals inspire you to take action, guide your focus to complete a task being undertaken and spur you on.

In the story, we also saw that the woman's goal of being healed led her to spend all her money on doctors. When that didn't work, this goal of hers—to be healed—clearly propelled her to push through the crowd to touch the hem of Jesus's garment.

Similarly, my goal to become a police officer made me push myself to read several newspaper articles about political affairs and listen to local and international news. Frankly, I had absolutely zero interest in politics. The result was that I became knowledgeable about current affairs; consequently, not only did I pass the interview, but I was also able to make important life decisions from an informed point of view. The point I'm making is—it pays to have a goal! Tasks get completed, and things get done only when you take robust action.

3. If at first you don't succeed, try, try, and try again

Arguably, one of the most important lessons we can learn from the woman with the issue of blood is if at first you don't succeed, try, try, and try again. Be persistent! She had suffered from her bleeding for twelve years. Imagine that! Numerous doctors couldn't cure her. She kept on trying, again and again. Upon hearing about Jesus, she tried yet once more. Her many failed attempts did not put her off trying again, and this time she was successful—she received her healing at last. Being persistent had paid off.

Equally, by that point in my life, I'd had many failed attempts at various things—not just the first interview. I had even normalized failure, believing that was my life. That was just the way it was.

You see, I was still young, trying to figure out who I was. However, I had the determination to succeed, and I kept trying. Persistence made me a police officer. When I was unsuccessful at the first interview, I went straight back. I nurtured my mind with great thoughts, convinced that I would never go any higher than I could think. In a quote attributed to Thomas Edison, the great inventor reminds us that “Many of life’s failures are people who did not realize how close they were to success when they gave up.” So never give up; try and try and try again.

Chapter 4
Christmas in November

I am not bound to win, but I am bound to be true. I am not bound to succeed, but I am bound to live up to what light I have.

—Attributed to Abraham Lincoln

My police academy training had finally ended. I was assigned to a specialized operational unit in the country's capital. A large contingent of us—probationers, as we were called—lived part-time in the barracks. We called it home.

Our unit had the responsibility of controlling or suppressing civil disturbances throughout the island. It was pure bliss. I felt like a young superhero, tied in with a little Wild Explorer somewhere in there too.

In the post, I traveled the entire island while on duty. Before this, I knew no other world apart from the community in which I grew up. Visiting other places had been relegated to a mere dream. Poverty did its utmost best and saw to it that I stayed put. Did someone say, "Best job ever!"?

I'm not sure how much was on my bucket list back then, but I do recall having the burning desire to visit various attractions on the island and get a first-hand experience of the country's rich culture and heritage. One morning in November 1990, I would be given such an experience, but not exactly how I had anticipated.

The glorious sunlight descended upon the grounds of the compound that housed the unit. As the day appeared promising, I felt full of energy, reporting for duty at the guardroom and hoping to be called into *action*. I was so ready to perform whatever task came in.

About half an hour had elapsed when the sub-officer on duty informed me an assignment had come in. Two other officers and I were deployed to the Jamaica Defence Force (JDF) to carry out an operation.

No further information was given at that point, but I knew that meant I needed to take my handbag. No, not the one you might be thinking. I'm talking about my rifle.

Speed was a key attribute when called for an operation. I hurriedly requested a firearm from the armoury and was issued with an M16 rifle. I checked and rechecked the ammunition to ensure I had, in fact, been issued the correct number of rounds. A mistake in that area could be fatal, not to mention that I could face disciplinary action if I failed to hand over or account for what I was issued.

I guarded my weapon with my life, as we were required to be armed on all duties. The truth, however, was that sometimes the responsibility of carrying a weapon was overbearing. I wished I didn't always need one, albeit whenever I was in possession of one, I felt powerful, armed, and dangerous!

My emotions were now bubbling like a pot of soup. Quite frankly, I was anxious. But I was over the moon to get this assignment. My assumption was that we would be off-site with the soldiers most of the day. It was an opportunity, my opportunity to put my training into practice at last.

To commence the assignment, two other officers and I went trekking to the JDF compound, taking a shortcut via an open field separating the JDF from the police compound. As we hurried along, I noticed the sparkling morning dew lighting up the grassy field like a colony of fireflies.

I've always been a mouth breather; my mouth was slightly ajar as I trod along. The rising sun caused a division of armed flies to swarm into the air. No doubt, as I inhaled and exhaled the fresh morning breath, a few flies flew in the path of my lips—good riddance!

We finally reached the compound and gathered in a room to learn detailed information about the job—a JDF-led operation. The purpose of having police officers ride along was chiefly to make arrests, if necessary, as soldiers do not have the power of arrest.

This was my first assignment. I understood very little, if any, of the jargon used, but hey, I pretended. *Fake it until you make it*, they say.

A true patriot, I was immensely proud. An opportunity was granted for me to do something positive for my country. My dream had become a reality; happy I was. For seven months of training, I'd been decked in police garb yet never once got the feeling like the one I had that morning. That realization kept me motivated and focused.

They shouted, “Ready, c’mon!” It was now time. On a large, open, grassy airfield, a helicopter was waiting. I hopped in unsuspectingly, after which it dawned on me: *We are traveling by air!*

This was my very first time flying. I wonder if my facial expressions were a dead giveaway. My heart’s content; I was like a child being taken out for a ride on daddy’s new bike. I had great expectations and planned on making it a day to remember.

Our party consisted of four soldiers—a pilot, a copilot, and two other men—and a police party. The latter consisted of two men and me. It came to a total of seven service personnel.

We sat close together, somewhat akin to sardines in a tin. The space was small, smack in the middle of the helicopter. In hindsight, compared to the passenger planes I’m now accustomed to, I should never have felt safe.

Two soldiers sat in the rear, and the pilot and copilot occupied the cockpit. I, however, was sandwiched between my fellow officers. Being the only female and the youngest in age and service on board never daunted me. I listened attentively to the safety instructions while ensuring I complied with all that was applicable. I felt appreciated and protected.

During the demo, the copilot told us we were going to debark in midair. I don’t know if this information was shared previously, but it was the first time I heard that bit. Blindsided, I felt my eyes bulge in disbelief.

“Midair? Are you serious?” I asked, mouth agape. “You mean we are going to leave the chopper while it’s still in the air?” I tried probing.

"Yes, we won't land. I'll lower the chopper, and you jump."

"I'll jump from the air?" I reemphasized.

"Yes, where we're going, there is no place to land. The airfield is a little way from the target, and if we land, we'll defeat our mission."

I knitted my brows in horror.

The pilot continued to explain the reason for their decision.

"I can't jump from a height. I've not done this before," I moaned.

"Don't worry. You'll jump for the first time today. The men will go first. Just watch what they'll do, and you do the same. You'll be OK."

My heart sank. *Should I ask to be excused from the operation?*

The copilot assured us the helicopter had been inspected, the straps were secure, and there was no safety issue.

I suspected that the other officers were anxious, even more than I was, but managed to mask their fears. Their eyes told the story.

It was now time to commence our journey, and mixed emotions engulfed me.

This was a day of firsts—my first operation, my first time setting foot in the JDF compound—a place I'd longed to behold and experience, given its all-important functions: the country's main security arm. It was my first time flying and also my first anticipated arrest.

When the rotor blades started turning, I was surprised at how noisy it was inside. Thank goodness for the intercom headset. I was able to hear the pilots and could talk with them if I wanted to.

The helicopter ascended like an eagle against the wind. The bustling of early-morning city life faded away. The tooting of horns and the revving up of engines from the rush hour could no longer be heard. A sea of schoolers decked in their diversified and colorful uniforms ebbed away too. Hurrying to their place of work, the many people on foot became like grasshoppers and soon vanished from my sight.

Wow! We climbed into an altitude of serenity. I watched the captivating clouds slide over the crystal-blue sky. My bird's-eye view of the masterful design of this place on earth called home almost blew my mind. This majestic sight of the country's landscape was something to behold. My eyes became affixed to the never-ending central display of natural beauty and grandeur.

The helicopter climbed higher and higher into the blustering wind. It was like sitting in a cinema where my eyes were drawn automatically to the screen as the movie rolled.

A blanket of white, fluffy clouds, green alpine-like trees, blue sandy beaches, and ocean-depth waves canvassed the earth.

For the first time, I saw vividly the various indentations of the Jamaica land mass, which was held in place within the boundaries of the sea. God, the Architect of this universe, is truly amazing!

One of my unforgettable moments was when I beheld the famous Vere Plain, which boasts a piece of land resembling the head and neck of an inverted crow. I was amazed at how accurately the map of Jamaica depicted the reality of the country's land mass.

The sight of the endless beauty that spread out before me was spectacular indeed! My heart was enlightened, and I was drawn into a deeper appreciation of the gift of life and the privilege of sight.

This awesome creation could only have been designed by the omnipotent, omnipresent, omniscient God of heaven. This experience still resonates with me today.

For most of the flight, silence descended on the chopper, and all seven passengers seemed engrossed in their personal conversations with nature.

Situated on the west coast of the island, our target was an approximately thirty-minute flight. Soon the copilot directed our attention to our target, and we scanned it from a distance. It was a small, isolated house. The pilot tipped the chopper on its side to ensure we all had a clear view of key points. The house then disappeared as the chopper began its descent.

"Get ready! Get ready!" the copilot commanded.

Suddenly a buzz started among the party, and the chopper door opened. One soldier sat in the doorway with his legs hanging outside. I took up my rifle and slung it around my neck in preparation for my air debark.

"Go! Go! Go!" the next command came.

One by one, the men flew out of the helicopter in quick succession, like birds escaping from a cage.

I remembered that in our assault training, jumping from heights was a key aspect of the course. But that was nothing in comparison to what I was about to do.

I tried to recall all the guidance given in that course, like breaking my fall, not landing flat-footed, and bending my hips and knees to the squatting position to soften the landing.

As the fourth man flew out of the chopper, without hesitation, I followed.

One, two, three, and out, I jumped. It happened so quickly I didn't have time to think or panic. My landing was pretty good, actually. But the blustery wind from the chopper nearly tipped me over as I tried to run as I landed.

I swung the rifle into position and started moving like a cheetah going for its prey. I wanted to catch up with the party, as they were now a good distance ahead—everyone moving at jet speed, not a minute wasted—like a combat scene in an action movie.

Glancing ahead, I saw the soldiers' gear blended into the bushes, creating a kind of camouflage. Not so much the officers, though. We were wearing blue denim shirts and trousers that stood out like a sore thumb.

The party made its way out of the bushes and came alongside a barbed-wire fence about 150 yards long and 13.5 yards high. It was the fencing around our target. The men ran to the gate and snooped about the house; they kicked in doors while shouting, "Police! Police! Who's inside? Don't move." I didn't enter by the gate. I scaled the fencing and landed in the yard.

As I tried to reach the house where the men were, I noticed I was sinking in white beach sand, although there was no beach nearby. My curiosity was piqued; I wanted to know the reason the area was so damp and sandy and why my feet were disappearing under the sand with every step. It was like walking on a huge wet sponge or, more accurately, walking on quicksand.

It drew the attention of the party; that area became the focus of our attention for the duration of the operation. Not a soul was at home, and the house appeared partially unoccupied. I'm not sure if, at our approach, anyone fled.

The party decided to dig up the sandy area of the yard to see if anything was hidden below. Due to not having the appropriate tools, the men improvised by using whatever implement they found. Fortuitously, they found shovels and other gardening tools.

We dug and dug, and it soon became evident that a hole had been covered up by the sand. It was not long before we discovered a metal container planted in the earth.

The men started singing chirpily, chanting as if cheering on their team at a football game. I tried to make sense of their enthusiasm, but it was not evident at the time.

Soon they started shouting, "Christmas!" (stretching out the "a" into a very long sound). "Christmas! Christmas." They laughed and talked among themselves.

I heard some say, "Christmas comes early," as they began removing some neatly wrapped packages from the hole. The packages were bound several times with brown packing tape. I learnt they were compressed marijuana for export, apparently.

But still, I remained puzzled as to the sudden exuberance.

Christmas in November?

Was this a code or jargon I hadn't yet learnt?

Evidently, it was a huge drug bust. It turned out that they'd dug up a metal drum buried in the earth, which contained approximately fifty packages of compressed weed, each package weighing about 11 pounds.

It was time to head back to base. The raid was successful, although we made no arrests. I felt happy to have tasted victory.

To transport the packages to the chopper, we divided them among ourselves. We loaded them in the tail and took up our positions in the chopper, the same as before. We headed back to our base in Kingston, stopping en route to refuel at Sangster International Airport in Montego Bay, the country's second city.

It was near dusk when we arrived—my stomach grumbling and my legs weary. My denim was sweaty, and my eyes wanted to rest. But the thought lingered in my head: *Why Christmas in November?* Asking what was next, I was told: head back to base, hand in my rifle, and the rest of the evening was mine.

In preparation for separation, we began gathering our personal stuff. One of the soldiers shouted, "Hey!" to grab our attention.

He flung some packages of weed at my colleagues as though he were playing a game of cricket—the packages were the ball and the policemen the wicket. They caught them on their chest, as a footballer would control a ball with his chest. Then quickly hid them under their denim shirts, making it like a barrier around their torso.

Unbeknownst to me, it was now my turn. A package came like a bullet towards me, and I quickly dodged it, as I would the ball in a game of dandy shandy or dodgeball.

As in cricket, a second package came flying towards my chest like a ball toward the wicket. Again, I eased sideways, allowing it to fly past my shoulder, landing on the airfield where we were. All the men were stunned at my reaction.

"The policewoman dodging gold!" one of my fellow officers remarked. My eyes opened wide, and I imagined my face told of my naivety.

One of my colleagues tried desperately to get me on board. "Officer, you don't want Christmas money?" he probed.

It then became clear why earlier they were shouting, "Christmas, Christmas."

"I don't want that stuff. What am I doing with it?" I asked with great annoyance.

"Take it and sell it. It's worth a lot of money." He tried to tempt me.

"No, I'm not doing it. I don't want it. I'll have nothing to do with it. I prefer to stay away from those things," I protested.

Nevertheless, my colleague was relentless in trying to persuade me to accept at least one of the packages.

I was astonished at the wanton disregard for Force policies, laws, and morals. I was firm that I was not going to participate in corruption.

But I felt pressured, scared, and anxious about the potential ripple effect of not accepting any. It appeared the men began to fear I might snitch on them.

"Let me tell you what I can do for you. I will take your share, sell it, and give you the money. Nobody will know about it, then," the officer pressed.

It was evident that this policeman wasn›t gonna leave me out of his destructive plans. The sum of money he said I could get was about ten times my monthly salary.

How impressive, I thought. I would be able to buy some furniture to start setting up my own home, then move out of my humble family shack.

It would be an opportunity to *show off*, to impress my neighbors and friends, letting them believe that life had really turned around for me; I now had it good.

In the same breath, I thought about the charge that was given to us during training by Mr. McKnight, the stern commanding officer. He warned us not to become rogue cops and not to bring the name of the Force into disrepute.

Mr. McKnight admonished us to be of good repute, strong to walk away from temptations, and not to take part in bribery and corruption. He warned us that temptations would come, but we must stand for honesty and integrity, even if it meant we were standing alone. Failure to do so would put us into a place where concrete would be our bed and pillow, he advised us.

Not only was the warning a solemn reminder, but it also painted a picture of being incarcerated and leaving my two sons behind. How could I do this corrupt thing and let down my children, family, and myself again?

It was indeed a day of firsts. My first encounter with corruption. What had started out as a day of happiness and excitement ended with torment and frustration. Never in my wildest dream would I have thought I would encounter blatant corruption so early in my career. My first operation.

After that encounter, I walked slowly to our base, feeling tired and drained, not only physically but mentally too.

In the days that followed, the same policeman kept coming to my barrack to check on me. He wanted to know how I was coping, given that encounter. I believe he was trying to befriend me to ensure I kept silent about their deviant behavior. I had no intention of whistleblowing. I was too fearful I would be pulled into a battle I had no strength to fight. I just wanted to stay clear of corruption and be left alone by those officers.

Within a few weeks of the operation, news broke not only at my unit but within the entire JCF that I was being transferred to the Hanover Division, the other side of the island, and the Force *dumping ground*.

What happened? "What have you done?" was the question on everyone's lips.

I was stunned or rather devastated about this transfer. I did not request one and was taken by surprise. Almost everyone else was surprised too.

Up to that time, I'd only visited the parish of Hanover once, and it did not leave a good impression. There, life appeared dated, behind the times. It was as if at the beginning of civilization, as I understood it from my history classes.

The communities I visited were deep rural villages. I recalled it was a treacherous journey from Palmers Cross, Clarendon, where I lived, to there. The roads in Hanover were steep, narrow, and winding. It seemed as if those who designed it were paid per mile. Therefore, the more miles built into a journey, the better their paycheck. It must be, as there were no other obvious reasons the roads were so dangerously dragged out, especially in the countryside.

Farming was one of the main occupations, with sugar cane the choice crop. Farm and woodlands featured prominently. So, I imagined the roads were designed to accommodate mainly tractors. Therefore, the potholes, which had become unattended little ponds, appeared not to be a big deal to residents.

As you might imagine, I was just getting accustomed to progressive city life, and I had high hopes and dreams for my kids, my family, and myself. For a long time, poverty had been calling out my name. I dreaded returning to a point worse than my humble beginning.

Evidently, I was not willing to join the naughty bunch, so they plotted against me. I thought I might have been perceived as a snitch, even though I had not reported on anyone. Nevertheless, I believe I had become a *thorn in the flesh*.

In my pursuit of an explanation for my transfer and to have that decision overturned, I went to the police federation, the body responsible for our welfare. But it was to no avail. I was told they were advised to expect me to call on them, but the transfer would not be canceled. It would be best, they suggested, if I took up the transfer.

Therefore, whoever had orchestrated my transfer had done everything to ensure that I left not only the unit I was assigned to but that entire geographical region.

It was a difficult situation because I was only twenty years old, a single mother of two young children, going to a strange place to reside and work. I had no friends or family networks in that parish.

I could not commute to Palmers Cross daily, given the long distance and very poor public transport system. Furthermore, I did not own a car—a distant reality. As a matter of fact, I could not drive then. My means of transport was my two legs. No wonder I was slim and fit. If I had not been resilient, I could have suffered various degrees of isolation.

After all, I was still emerging from a life of privation. It is well documented that teen mums face emotional and mental distress. The only constants in my life had been fear and worry, regret and frustration, guilt, shame, and disruption.

I did not want to battle with isolation too. I was worried it would have crippled me. Inadequate support would exacerbate the challenges I would face on my own as a teen mother and a police officer. I needed support on many issues, such as childcare, finances, education, and the multiple needs of my children.

I envisaged that the increased responsibilities would be overwhelming and could push me over the edge.

Although my family was broken and scattered, they were still near me and my children if I needed them. This was a source of comfort. Though we were disconnected sometimes, they were still my family, and I still loved them. I wanted to be near them.

Not to mention my friends, though few. Not having access to them was likely to increase the strain and test my coping ability. My friends acted as an important form of social support.

Nevertheless, I was determined to defy the odds. This was another hurdle to surmount. I believed that God would work something out for me.

This situation reminded me of the story in the Bible, where God told Abram to leave his country, family, and relatives and go to a faraway land he knew nothing about (Genesis 12:1).

In hindsight, due to my fear of the unknown, I did not meditate on the blessings promised to Abram in the following verse (Genesis 12:2). I should have seen my situation from the point of view that my transfer could be a blessing too. Indeed, in many respects, it was.

At the appointed time, I took up the transfer to the then-remote, rural, undeveloped parish called Hanover. I reasoned that most of the *bad cops* were supposedly sent there. Therefore, it could not be a good place.

Little did I know that it was God who had intervened at that juncture and redirected me to a place where he would launch me into my purpose for that season.

Regarding the transfer, one colleague said to me, "Girl, you must have done something very bad to be sent to Hanover. Only a police station, a post office, and a shop make up the town!"

I felt he was exaggerating, but I got his message. It wasn't far from the point he was trying to convey. That is, I was banished, dumped, to a forgotten place. What would I do with my life there? Being transferred to Hanover was akin to John of Patmos being exiled to the Aegean Sea island in the Bible.

Ye of little faith!

I cried until my eyes were swollen. I could barely see out of them. I knew my transfer was a plot to get rid of me.

Takeaways

1. Honesty is the best policy

You must practice honesty in every setting, including your workplace. God will bless you abundantly. Always do the right thing, even if you are the only person doing what is right. *Honesty is the best policy*. Imagine living in fear of being caught, losing your job, tarnishing your character, or suffering humiliation because you stole something from work. Think about the negative impact on your children, family, and loved ones. Remember, "*Ill-gotten gain gets you nowhere; an honest life is immortal*" (Proverbs 10:2 MSG). The NLT version puts it this way: "Tainted *wealth has no lasting value, but right living can save your life.*"

2. God is in control of every situation

Believe that God is always in full control, and He knows what's best for you. The Serenity Prayer by Reinhold Niebuhr, an American theologian, says, "God, grant me the serenity to accept the things I cannot change, courage to change the things I can, and the wisdom to know the difference." Reflect on this prayer. Recognizing what you can't change—the things you have no control over—placing your focus on what you can control and submitting the rest to God is key to having contentment.

3. **Do not fear, worry or fret!**

Fear robs us of rational thinking and can lead us to make poor decisions. I read a quote that says, "The cave you fear to enter holds the treasures you seek." God promises to guide us in every situation we face. In Isaiah 43.1 KJV, He says, "Fear not, for I have redeemed you; I have called you by your name; you are Mine." So, my advice to you is: be calm in difficult situations. Remember, God has your back!

Chapter 5
The Passion in Me

A pessimist sees the difficulty in every opportunity; an optimist sees the opportunity in every difficulty.

—Winston Churchill

Life is a journey with many encounters, some of which change the trajectory of our lives. Though I dreaded going to Hanover and tried everything in my power not to, the reality was—real growth began there. Had I remained in Kingston, I would have thwarted some of the many blessings that awaited me—including discovering one of my passions—although some of those blessings did not come in attractively wrapped packages.

I remember it was a calm, sunny midmorning in December 1990 when I hesitantly stuffed my bags and pans into the boot of a police car en route to the parish of Hanover, which I would later call home.

Standing in one of the parking bays on the compound, looking around, I viewed for the last time the barracks and other buildings, the site of what was once my revered place of work, where I first experienced life as a policewoman.

As I reflected on what my next assignment would be like, a great sense of weariness swept over me, sucking my energy and dulling my eyes with sadness.

Quietly, I took my seat in the rear of the vehicle, indicating I was ready to go.

"Are you ready, my lady?" the driver—a sergeant—inquired while settling himself at the steering wheel.

Blinking away the tears and with a lump in my throat, I muttered, "I am, sir."

"Are you sure you have everything?"

"I think so, sir."

The escort, a corporal, seated himself in the front passenger seat, evidently upbeat about the trip. I held my breath, hoping he did not attempt to engage me in conversation, having taken note of my *DO NOT DISTURB* sign displayed all over my face. A slight squint and the fountain of tears edging my eyelids would overflow—revealing my internal reality.

We slowly drove up to the sentry gate. The guard peered into our car, then raised the long metal barrier stretched across the gateway. The vehicle rolled out of the compound, commencing my journey to the *forgotten* parish situated on the northwestern tip of the island.

Convinced in my thoughts that I was leaving behind a presumably prosperous, charming city life for a remote, unprogressive, joy-killing, backward place, I thought my career had ended before it even began.

We navigated through lightly sprinkled traffic, exiting the city, entering sweeter air with notably greener trees, animals grazing, and rivers flowing. In my extreme duress, refusing to converse with either of my colleagues about the transfer, I opted to converse with nature instead—becoming drawn by long stretches of hillside glowing green in the light of the bright mid-morning sun, coaxing my inner energy that flowed in ways that wove some peace into my soul.

The distance appeared as though we were going from one corner of the globe to the next—a never-ending journey!

As we traveled, my two colleagues were locked into various conversations, splattered with random bursts of laughter. They were certainly enjoying the trip—unlike me.

With my eyes closed, I tried to visualize the destination, napping intermittently. After about two rounds, and like a child going on an adventure, I kept on asking, in a silent tone, "Are we there yet? How long before we get there?"

Finally, after about three and a half hours of nonstop traveling, we pulled into the small colonial town of Lucea, the capital of Hanover, situated on the edge of a huge bay. Featuring colonial homes, it looked out to an aquamarine sea.

Lucea had been a banana and sugar port of trade until the 1980s. Hanover is a part of the county of Cornwell, bordering St. James in the east and Westmoreland in the south. It is one of Jamaica's smallest parishes.

The town boasts several ancient buildings, the kind you would see in some medieval movies. The police station, though, was a more modern structure with an untinted glass wall across the front and on one side of the ground floor. Not so ideal, I would say—considering the nature of the job. I believe the building was more eco-friendly than purpose-built.

Reflecting on the building brings to mind the lyrics from the hit by the late Peter Tosh, a reggae singer, "If you live in a glass house, don't throw stones."

However, as we pulled up to the front of the station, a female corporal, her rank at the time, came over to greet us. Obviously, on the lookout for us, she had been standing at the front door, the entrance to a small reception area on the ground floor of the building.

Coming up to us, she introduced herself as the Divisional Training Sub-officer (DTSO)—having responsibility for the probationer's training and development. She would be my main supervisor for the remainder of my probationary period, a little under two years.

With thank-yous and brief chit-chat out of the way, the driver and escort wished me a productive stay, unloaded my stuff from the car, and bid us goodbye.

The DTSO and other officers, welcoming me, gave me a tour of the station before taking me to a colonial-structured house along the seafront—a house owned and occupied by an elderly lady, Mrs. Johnson, probably in her mid-seventies. Her daughter, her husband, and two grandchildren lived there too.

Warmly, with hospitality, Mrs. Johnson showed me around the house. It had the feel and decor of a typical grandma's residence. The bedroom I would occupy had a double bed and basic furniture, with a glimpse of the sea and traffic in and out of the town square.

Inviting me to dinner, Mrs. Johnson took me to her open-plan kitchen/dining room. With steam oozing through the pots and their lids, sitting on the cooker, she started dishing up some flavoursome food.

Frankly, though, a ride to Clarendon, my home parish, would have been the only appetizing thing for me that evening. Nothing had meaning that entire day and night. I felt dumped, rejected, and confused. I longed for home and my children, whom I'd left in the care of their grandmothers.

I remember—contemplating how to get back home—going onto the veranda upstairs, looking out onto the wide-open grayish-blue sea, spitting up its froth in the wind beneath the lush green mountain line in the not-too-far distance. I added up in my head the many miles, given that I lived on the other side of the island, closer to Kingston. Public transportation was not prevalent in those days, and I was away from home.

Directly across from the house lay the sea—only the main road that led to the town square separating it from the sea. The road and the sea appeared to be on the same level but parted by a thick retaining wall about three feet high, evidently a footpath for many.

A door creaking open, and footsteps on the veranda broke my deep reverie.

"Are you okay, Miss Cunningham?" with a sense of curiosity, Mrs. Johnson inquired.

"How do I get to Clarendon from here?" I asked.

"That's a very long way to go. But you can travel through Montego Bay—the way you came—or through Westmoreland, the other end.

"Why do you ask? You're not planning to go there now, are you? Mrs. Johnson probed.

"That's where I'm from. I just need to know how to get home."

"Okay, but are you going there tonight?"

"No, Mrs. Johnson, not tonight—but soon," I asserted, with more certainty than I felt.

Mrs. Johnson rightly assessed that I was not in any mood for a conversation. She invited me to talk with her when I'd had some time to think, then excused herself and went to the kitchen/dining area. I went to my bedroom, shut the door, and threw myself onto the bed, burying my face into the pillow. I bawled—not cried! I bawled and bawled.

"Miss Cunningham, are you okay?" Mrs. Johnson's voice came through the closed bedroom door."

"I'm okay," I just barely managed to answer, faintly, after a few seconds.

"Come and have something to drink. You're from far away, and you haven't eaten dinner. You're not alone. A lot of people have come here for the first time and didn't like it either. But after a while, they grew to love it. You could not remove them, even with a bulldozer."

"Not me!" I mumbled, annoyed.

I imagined Mrs. Johnson thinking that as a policewoman, I had come here to protect, reassure, and serve the citizens. But in a sense, the reverse was true. I retired to bed early that evening, hoping to sleep my sorrows away.

The following morning, I rose with great determination to push aside the worry and frustration that had plagued me since finding out about the transfer.

As the days passed, I told myself I was in Hanover. There was nothing I could do, so it made sense—didn't it?—to get on with the business at hand. The good thing was I had a job and was in good health.

I reflected that one of the lessons the caterpillar taught us was that change can be a beautiful thing. The butterfly was first a fussy, creepy, hairy insect that metamorphosed to become that beautiful soft, colored, winged insect. When it was a caterpillar, its reach was localized—it wasn't able to go far. But when it bursts from its cocoon and discovers it has wings, rather than hoping to one day turn back, it flies.

Being assigned to Lucea Police Station, the head station, meant doing a lot of foot patrol in the town square. I hated it because walking around made my feet swollen like jackfruit or balloons. Also, the colonial, heavily starched, hot, thick uniform shirt, evidently designed for cold weather, was no comfort in the scorching heat.

Nevertheless, whatever duty I performed, it afforded me the opportunity to interact with citizens on a meaningful level, unlike my previous assignment in Kingston, where we were engaged in what might be described as harsh policing.

In comparison to Kingston, working in Hanover was like a walk in the park. It being a quiet parish, I was not surprised to discover the warmth and friendliness of the people.

Soon, I developed a passion for community-based policing, that is, working in partnership with community groups (churches, schools, neighborhood watch groups, nongovernment organizations, etc.) to improve relationships and build confidence and trust in the police.

Feeling I could make a strong club leader, my supervisors assigned me to head up the almost-defunct Lucea police youth club. Unhesitantly, I accepted the task, even though I felt it was a challenging assignment. I saw it as an opportunity to make meaningful connections in the communities, to care for people, and to be a voice for youth.

Little did I know that this assignment was training for what the Lord had prepared for me more than twenty years in the future.

Trying to get the club up and running was like trying to manually jumpstart a dead, old car engine. As you can imagine, it involved making some connections and perhaps physically pushing the car too, but once it started, the car kept going—so with the youth club. Although I didn't have to physically push anything, motivating and encouraging members was just as taxing on the mind and body. Nevertheless, they were worth it!

Realizing I had a knack for youth work brightened my focus—gave me something I needed to aid in overcoming my own personal struggles. I was on a mission to help turn around the lives of less-fortunate youths. Steve Harvey, an American comedian, TV host, actor, and author, is quoted as saying: "Do not ignore the passion that burns in you. Spend time to discover your gift." I had just discovered one of mine!

Given my own experiences as a youth, it was easy to spot troubled youngsters, some of whom I managed to convince to join the club. And for whom the club became their safe haven.

We started with a few youths, ages twelve to twenty years old, males and females. Eventually, the number swelled. I can't remember the exact number on the roster, but perhaps about forty to fifty, with more than half in regular, weekly attendance.

Upon the formation of a proper club structure and election of officers, including a secretary and a finance officer, we were on a mission to unite and impact Lucea and surrounding communities in a marked way.

When it came to community projects and activities, the youth were like energizer bunnies: they kept going and going. We accomplished one task after the other, much to the delight of the community or agencies involved.

Oprah Winfrey is credited with reminding us that "Every time a child is saved from the dark side of life, every time one of us makes the effort to make a difference in a child's life, we add light and healing to our own lives." The biggest mistake in helping underserved kids is *not* raising the bar high enough. Children will believe if you believe in them.

As such, it was important that, in order to positively impact and affect change in their communities, all the youth felt valued and listened to. Making myself available not only during but outside of the club's operating hours and my working hours proved an empowering avenue for dealing with some of the issues faced by them.

The club came under the umbrella of the National Police Youth Club, an arm of the then Community Relations Branch located in Kingston. That meant we had the backing from higher command, making us more accepted and effective in our efforts.

The club grew immensely, but not only the youth benefitted. I grew too. It was like the springtime of that career, I would say. Similarly, to how rain waters the earth, making plants sprout and blossom, growing seeds for the farmer and food for others, so did my work produce results.

Some of these testimonials are in Part Two of this book, including one from a then-youth, Andrew, who went on to become a police officer and elder in a local church, rescuing many youths from a life of crime.

It is fitting to mention here that I developed effective youth work skills, including in communication and behavioral management—learning to decipher what the youth were communicating, not only by words but even by some unpleasant behavior. These skills would prove vital in my future career. I like to think I was like a big sister to the club members, somewhat modeling the big-sister program I benefited from at TMP.

The club's activities included a yearly summer camp where we hosted the Miss Police Youth Club—a talent show, the highlight of summer camp; and national sports day, which always followed the Police National Sports Day—a major calendar event.

Community projects included visiting the children's home in the parish—bringing hope and encouragement to children—and competing in the national festival talent show—a way of developing and promoting the creative talents and cultural expressions of the club members. The finalists were the crème de la crème.

May I proudly say that one year we placed first runner-up—a great achievement of ours. Recalling it still fills my heart with pride and joy. The club member we selected to represent us did a captivating rendition of the Whitney

Houston hit "I Will Always Love You." I believe Whitney, listening, would have thought she was cloned.

That was a huge success for the club, motivating many others to join and work on developing their giftedness. To further this, we hosted a massive concert in the parish, showcasing the members' various talents.

The concert was attended by people from all strata of life: the resident magistrate, lawyers, teachers, bankers, hoteliers, justices of the peace, police, politicians, and political influencers, just to name a few. As a matter of fact, everybody who was anybody attended. Probably, it was the largest community event of its kind in the history of the parish at that time. The business community and political influencers were overjoyed to witness the police and citizenry coming together in such unity.

A very influential businessman, Mr. Wilson, aka *Try Me*, the top justice of the peace at the time, remarked, "This is the kind of activity and togetherness we want to see in our parish. It's good for the people of Hanover."

Such an event was a major one for the parish at the time. Afterwards, I learnt that the police superintendent's office line was flooded with commendations for the police.

Evidently, the social and educational development of the club members improved. None of them were known for antisocial behavior; school attendance improved, some found gainful employment, and others pursued higher education. I became known as the face of the community relations unit in my division.

Two persons became life partners, having met at the club, fallen in love, and subsequently married. Their union has produced children, and their marriage is still going strong today. The wife is now a general nurse. She expressed being blessed by their experiences and skills gained in the club. It equipped them to successfully navigate life's challenges.

Unfortunately, while the community's love and appreciation for the tremendous youth work I was doing was growing, paradoxically, the reverse was happening in the Force, or—to be more specific—in my division.

Evil rose its ugly head. I began getting some of the worst duties, including being placed on lots of night shifts, especially *graveyard* shifts (midnight to 8:00 a.m.). It was well known that those shifts were used as punishment for female constables.

By now, my firstborn, seven years old, lived with me. I hired a nanny who cared for him when I was at work. Due to cost constraints, we operated a kind of shift rota. But sometimes, I had no one to babysit.

My two choices then were either to bring my son to work or to be absent from work and suffer the backlash. The reality was I had limited support. You might guess correctly what I did. If you guess the former, then you are correct.

Having learnt the art of juggling parenting, school, and career, I was in good stead. We did not have the luxury of a nursery at work.

Making good use of daytime freedom from work, I enrolled in evening school. Joe Biden, US president, says, "A job is about a lot more than a paycheck. It's about your dignity. It's about respect. It's about your place in your community." I felt I needed formal education to help me in my decision-making, self-awareness, career progression, and life purpose. I started in pursuit of at least a secondary education—my way of unlocking opportunity's doors.

Resitting for my General Certificate of Education (GCE) and Caribbean Examinations Council (CXC) exams, I was determined to give myself that solid education my mother had hoped for me.

Often cited as an Oprah Winfrey quote: "Education is the way to move mountains, to build bridges, to change the world. Education is the path to the future." I believe that education is indeed freedom.

The nights were usually quiet—creating the perfect study atmosphere. I transformed the guard room into a mini study where I *beat the books* throughout the night. By the end of a shift, I felt like a walking encyclopedia. I was ahead in my lessons.

Being successful in my GCE and CXC exams and gaining distinctions and credits, I *was* moved to apply to go to university. However, how could I get a leave from work? No one in my division had ever been granted this leave before. Actually, not many people were aware of this opportunity. Nonetheless, in 1997 after many difficulties and disappointments, personally and professionally, I applied for three years of study leave.

Fortunately, a colleague from the general office (division of resources) had applied also. She kindly outlined the process to follow to ensure the file reached its final destination by the deadline.

As such, I needed to hand-deliver the file to the different offices in the channel, reaching the Ministry of National Security, the body that grants the approval.

It so happened that, a day after the Inspector in charge of the station submitted the application to the general office, the file—mysteriously—could not be found. Those were the days of paper files. However, following a deep search of the office, the file was located hidden away.

Who did it? I don't know, it was not made clear, but it doesn't matter now. What was evident was that person's desire to stop me from going off to university. That was just evil, period!

In hindsight, I realized that God knew the scheming and plotting of Satan to block my blessings. Therefore, He went ahead, clearing the path by sending my colleague to alert me to chase up the file. Had that not happened, I would be none the wiser and would have missed out on a glorious opportunity to further my education. It pays to trust God!

I am now convinced that one of the reasons God condoned my transfer to the parish was to favor me with His blessings of higher education. Therefore, the evil scheming could not have been successful. God knew my learning was for His glory—even though I was not clear about His plan for my life then.

Through the youth work, many lives were turned around for good. Parent-child relationships improved, giving parents renewed hope in their children. As a matter of fact, in some cases, entire family relationships improved.

Reflecting on the experiences somewhat reminded me of the story of Joseph in the Bible. Although, by far, my experiences were by no means equivalent to Joseph's experiences, I nevertheless, through them, learnt some key lessons.

The story is found in the book of Genesis, chapters 37–50. Joseph, one of the twelve sons of the patriarch Jacob, was thrown into a pit by his jealous brothers, who intended to leave him to die. But later took him out and sold him into slavery. He was taken to Egypt and eventually became a steward to Potiphar, captain of Pharaoh's guard.

Initially, it was difficult for Joseph. Potiphar's wife even initially accused him of impropriety. Potiphar's other servants were jealous of his rise to prominence in their household, so they gave in to their jealousy by believing the wife's story. Joseph was thrown into prison. But God had a plan for him. He was promoted to prime minister of Egypt. God turned a sad situation into a miracle, saving many lives.

Although my situation was nowhere as dramatic as Joseph's, I was shipped off to a place that was intended to be a punishment. And I met grave challenges there, but actually, I found my passion through it all; that is, working with children and youth, giving them hope in seemingly hopeless situations, resulting in their lives being turned around.

In Joseph's story, though his transition was awful, God was right there with him. The scripture says, "But the Lord was with Joseph and showed him steadfast love and gave him favour…" (Genesis 39:21, ESV). God will do the same for you and me in our transitioning.

It was in the parish of Hanover I made a lifelong friend, Norvelet—one of the most genuine, kind, thoughtful, caring souls one could have as a friend.

Norvelet reintroduced me to church life and taught me many Christlike virtues. She helped me to fall in love with

Jesus again. Her love and encouragement nurtured me to recommit my life to Christ, which resulted in my rebaptism—the best decision I ever made.

As a matter of fact, it was in modeling Norvelet that I was motivated to pursue my first undergraduate degree. She was a tower of strength in many areas of my life, including being a special aunty, or rather an *unpaid nanny*, to my children. I'm forever grateful. Although we now live hundreds of miles apart, our friendship is still strong. I thank God for sending her into my life.

This bit I should really tell you. It was in the parish of Hanover that I bought my first dream home—a property I'm still in possession of, up to the time of writing this book.

I fell in love with Hanover parish, so much so that not even a bombing like that of Hiroshima or Nagasaki could uproot me! Mrs. Johnson was right after all, eh?

Takeaways

1. Learn to embrace change

Change could be a blessing in disguise. Change can allow us to move forward in life and experience new and exciting things, even some we didn't imagine were possible. For example, moving somewhere could be a transition that allows you to form new friendships or connections—change jobs or progress in your career—discovering a passion in you, as it did for me. I was able to have a positive impact on the lives of many youths and their families. When we embrace change, we learn coping strategies and build resilience.

2. Make the best of your situation

Accept where you are at the moment and make the best of it. Bawl if you have to like I did, but then pick yourself up and get on with it. When you try to change or deny things that you *can't* change, it results in anger or frustration, upsetting your emotional equilibrium. On the other hand, trust and acceptance will bring you peace and calm, eventually. Taking things as they are does not necessarily mean that you have to enjoy what's happening. It simply means you acknowledge that you don't have control over what's happening, and it is what it is.

3. Learn to make tough decisions

Sometimes in life, we have to make very tough decisions. I believe that how we make tough decisions, ultimately, is the difference between failure and success. Regarding resigning or taking up my transfer, I had to make really tough decisions that had childcare implications. What helped me was writing things down and evaluating them by looking at the possible outcomes—trying to lessen negative outcomes by being proactive. When things didn't turn out as expected, instead of seeing it as a failure, I viewed it as a learning experience and a springboard for starting something else.

Chapter 6
Plot to Destroy Me

Peace is not the absence of conflict,
but the ability to cope with conflict by
peaceful means.

—Ronald Reagan

It was the summer of 2000. I completed a diploma in business administration, with an emphasis on accounting, at the University of Technology (UTech), Kingston, Jamaica. A diploma then had the weight of a degree now.

The police force had granted me three years' study leave with pay—yes, you read correctly. Full pay! It was as if God opened up the windows of heaven and poured out on me blessings in copious measures!

The first two years I took at Montego Bay Community College, the final year on the campus of UTech. I was one of the pupils in the final cohort of the diploma program, which would then phase into the bachelorette program the next academic year. Completing an additional year would land me my dream academic pursuit at that time—a Bachelor of Science in Business Administration.

Anyhow, upon resuming work, I continued my educational pursuit, returning to university on a part-time basis.

This time to Northern Caribbean University, where I gained my first Bachelor of Science degree, making history in the parish by being the first policewoman to earn a degree.

The job of the police carries a huge responsibility, but somehow I had almost forgotten how to perform those duties. Below is a list of some of them at that time:

- Patrolling on foot in the town square, defusing violence, and ensuring the safety of all (Beat Duty)
- Responding to calls and requests from members of the public (Station Guard)
- Manually updating books and documents (Records duty)
- Conducting investigations, gathering evidence, taking statements from witnesses, and arresting suspects
- Interviewing suspects and victims
- Performing court duties
- Executing warrants and serving summons and subpoenas (Process duty)

The truth is, during those three years of study, I did not miss policing one bit. Apart from academic pursuits, university life offered me the opportunity to have fun and catch up on some of what I missed during my youth. The pranks, funny birthday parties, our own version of "Come Dine with Me," meaningless discussions that went on until the wee hours of the morning were a remedy to my soul.

I did not have the added pressure that goes with police work. I was just happy to be a student again. Being a teen mum meant I had to grow up quickly, spending little time having fun or socializing with peers, as youth ought to.

I treasured the experience of living on the university campus, sharing a unit with some wonderful young women.

Our unit was a three-bedroom flat occupied by nine of us. They were brilliant, energetic, warm, and fun-loving.

Most of them had little or no life experiences and were away from their parents and family for the very first time. Except for Shauna, who, during all her high-school years, had lived at a boarding school, then went straight into university. She was adorable, very driven, and admirable.

Being the oldest of them all, I saw these girls as my little sisters. As such, I played my role well as a big sister. It was the role I wanted my biological sisters to have played, but sadly it didn't happen the way I would have liked.

I have garnered much wisdom since becoming a police officer. With the benefit of hindsight, I realize how much I learnt and grew from my experiences. I shared those lessons with my newfound sisters so they would not make the same mistakes.

Being a student was a twofold blessing:

Firstly, it gave me rest from a hectic life.

Secondly, I completed my higher education.

Although I dropped out of high school, I was determined to achieve an education beyond the secondary level. I beamed with joy at having achieved this goal. It was one other item ticked off my bucket list.

Returning to work was an interesting experience. Some days were like a scene in an action film, and the reality that I might be injured or killed was once more a daily possibility.

In the police station, it was vital that I stayed alert to what was happening around me, enabling me to respond appropriately.

The noisy guardroom lent a striking contrast to the packed yet quiet lecture auditorium I'd become familiar with—a scene that occupied most of my day's routine throughout the course of my study.

Usually, people were going in and out, making reports and seeking advice. Likewise, the phone line stayed busy with inquiries about anything and everything. Moreover, there was a stationary police radio which was connected to a central system. It had a steady flow of conversations and messages that sometimes concerned my station or division and required swift action.

I returned to work, bursting with knowledge and ideas on how to successfully run a business. I believed some of the strategies, if implemented, could bring about an improved service. However, if you want to see changes and it is not led from the top, it will not happen—even if it's evident where improvement could be made to serve the community better.

At that time, I was a constable, the lowest rank. I knew that any attempt to make service adjustments would run up against institutional barriers. Therefore, I did what was within my power to do. Soon, I began to stand out again. Commendations, especially from other professionals and members of the public, were rolling in once more.

I sat for my promotional examination and moved upward to the rank of corporal. It was at this time I cupped the coveted award of Divisional Police Officer of the Year—*Top Cop Award*.

It was not long before I started to attract enemies again. Jealousy and envy continue to raise their ugly heads among my colleagues. I believe some of my coworkers weren't happy with my educational achievement and promotion.

Promotion was a big thing among members of the Force. For many, it was a significant source of motivation. Promotion was about not just an increase in wage but status, power, and authority and an increase in benefits, all of which contributed to a more comfortable lifestyle.

I sensed that there were unhealthy competitive personalities; therefore, I tried to stay away from workplace politics, dramas, and controversy. My focus was on building a legacy for my children, who had struggled so much in their young lives. I also focused on helping my family out of poverty and hardship.

Certain female colleagues, in particular, targeted me, unafraid to show their prejudices. Yet, I remained oblivious to the extent of the danger lurking. The Lord had to use a probationer to enlighten me.

One morning I reported to work, and a police constable, Marcia, who had recently deployed to our division fresh from the academy, began a conversation with me that left me astounded.

She remarked, "I don't know if you are aware of this, but ever since you came back from university, they [names withheld] have been chatting about you. Lots of negative things." I knitted my brows in disbelief.

She continued, "When you walk into the station, they smile and greet you nicely, and you get to chatting and laughing with them. But behind your back, they gang up and slaughter you."

The truth is, I was really unfazed by her observation. But then she stated, "So, I have been observing you because I wanted to see if there was any truth to what they've been chatting about. To the contrary, you've not lived up to any of that slander. I realized it's all envy and jealousy."

She advised me to keep my food secure, which then piqued my interest because it had to do with my health and security.

"Stop leaving your food around," she warned. "They don't like you, and they can easily hurt you." Scary stuff!

Sometimes at work, I purchased a takeaway lunch and ate it at the desk while working. I would eat a portion and save the rest for later on. I usually placed the remainder in a cupboard near my handbag. It was not secure, and any of my colleagues could easily access it if they wanted to.

I did not know if this was her personal view or was derived from conversations she'd heard. Whatever it was, it certainly led her to believe that my food was at some kind of risk.

This situation reminded me of the story in Acts 23, where over forty Jewish leaders had plotted to kill Paul. They even took an oath that they would not eat or drink until they killed him. Paul's nephew, hearing of the assassination plot, disclosed it to him. The Lord wrought an escape, whereby Paul was taken to Caesarea under heavy security that night instead of the following morning, thereby escaping those who were intent on doing him harm.

Similarly, the Lord used the constable to awaken me to the scheme to destroy me. Again, it dawned on me that I was working in a toxic environment. However, the Lord's protection over me continued, despite my failings.

The plot to destroy me became more evident when a senior colleague fabricated a story against me to ruin my career. I thank God for intervening and saving me, just as he did for Paul.

I learnt that when adversity strikes, I must trust God to protect me by His providence. I became more vigilant and alert to my own personal security. It was evident that the threats from within the organization outweighed even those on the outside.

Having successfully completed my degree, I could apply to the Accelerated Promotion Programme (APP), which was new at the time. The APP was launched to help fill potential managerial gaps in the officers' corp. The program was aimed at increasing the number of senior officers by promoting rank-and-file members after substantial and rigorous training.

Many, particularly those who did not have a degree and did not intend to pursue one, were disgruntled about it. At that time, not many members of the Force had a degree. It was not a requirement to join. The Force wanted to drive the planning and development of leaders from within the organization. The Accelerated Promotion Program was one way of doing so.

At that time, if I was successful in my application, I could be promoted to the rank of Assistant Superintendent (ASP) within two years. This was indeed a very short period to be elevated to ASP. As the program name suggested, it meant accelerated promotion.

Many of my colleagues asked, "Are you gonna apply for the accelerated promotion program?"

Some addressed me as *the Corporal with a degree*. I recall being tossed into the spotlight, possibly to be humiliated; for example, being suddenly called upon to do a public presentation for which I was not prepared.

They told me, "You're a university graduate. You should know how to do this."

Honestly speaking, sometimes I didn't remember I had a degree. However, those around me never forgot and would remind me at opportune moments. Was this because they appreciated my achievement? It didn't appear that way at all.

I believe my then-colleagues feared I would be promoted above them. Looking back, I see the Lord was preparing me for His work ahead, to which I shall return later. I took those unfortunate situations as training and preparation for bigger assignments.

Frankly, the more dirt that was thrown at me, the more I shook off, trampled on, and used to climb to higher heights. Giving up was not an option. Not since I was determined to defy the odds.

Another morning Marcia told me she had a family emergency. A few days later, she did not come to work. To account for her absence, she reported herself sick, but in fact, she wasn't. Back at work, she got a strong telling-off from the same woman sergeant who had falsely accused me of advising Marcia to report sick. Marcia told her—correctly—I was not behind her decision.

"You are following Cunningham [my maiden name]; she's gonna lead you astray."

Taken aback, Marcia tried her best to convince the sergeant that I had nothing to do with her decision, but the sergeant was unconvinced. Very concerned, Marcia said it was evident the sergeant wanted to build a case against me.

The truth is, I didn't even know Marcia had gone off on sick leave. Obtaining leave was challenging. Generally, sickness absence was abused within the Force, and it impacted the rotas. Many officers opted for sickness absence when they wanted to be off for one reason or another.

To say I was frustrated is an understatement. The underhandedness and toxicity in which I was working ate away my peace. So as one who is solution-focused, I decided to have a dialogue with the sergeant, my senior, with the view that we could reach a resolution and move forward—strengthening my coping ability.

Even though I knew the sergeant was plotting my destruction, I was determined to make peace, to approach her in a calm spirit. I was trying not to lose inner peace for anything whatsoever, even though my whole world seemed upset. I was determined to defy the odds.

With this view in mind, I had a discussion with the sergeant, outlining my frustrations caused by her allegations.

How dare I speak to her about her conduct!

Of course, this wasn't gonna go down well. It was fuel for an already-burning fire.

The sergeant was shocked to learn that I was aware of her plotting and scheming. Nevertheless, she did not deny what Marcia told me. However, she lied about the conversation we had and further accused me of making derogatory statements about her.

Following this, the sergeant reported to the inspector in charge of the station where we were assigned. Her aim was that I would face disciplinary charges by way of a court of inquiry. This was like a magistrate's court hearing. One of the outcomes from such a hearing could be a recommendation for a financial penalty or, in extreme cases, dismissal.

In an attempt to appease the sergeant, the inspector initiated the disciplinary proceeding. The sergeant even got two persons who had not been present to give witness statements and later testify that they saw and heard me making derogatory comments. *How lie thou art!!*

Evidently, this woman was on a mission to destroy me.

The disciplinary hearing was extremely protracted, taking approximately three stressful years to reach the final outcome.

When an officer has a court-of-inquiry case pending, he or she is not permitted to sit for promotional exams, be promoted, or go on vacation leave.

This situation really crippled me. I felt stagnant, stifled, silenced, and subdued. My predicament began to affect my personal life.

I wanted to travel abroad to obtain medical help for one of my sons. At the time, the help he needed was not readily available in Jamaica. Yet, I was not allowed to travel outside the country. Police personnel needed the commissioner's authorization to travel abroad. I could not have vacation leave, so I could not go abroad.

My son's medical needs were becoming dire. Nevertheless, Satan was relentless in his pursuit to destroy me. And as if I did not have enough trouble, while that disciplinary hearing was taking place, I was accused of another incident, which led to a second disciplinary hearing.

"When it rains, it pours."

One evening after work, passing by the station where I worked, I stopped to make a phone call. Mobile phones were not common then. One of my fellow corporals from the traffic department asked if I could assist in a matter.

He told me a fatal accident occurred that evening in Negril (adjoining parish), and some policemen had brought the driver suspect to be breathalysed. I was one of the breathalyser analysts for my division. However, the analyst on duty that evening claimed he had forgotten how to program the breathalyser machine in order to process the breath sample.

Being the helpful person, I was, I agreed to refresh the analyst on how to program the machine. This meant I had to travel approximately a mile and a half in the opposite direction from where I was going; nonetheless, I was happy to assist. I had no idea who the suspect was or the details of the accident.

Along with the analyst who was my junior, I went to the police headquarters, where the breathalyser machine was installed. I observed that there was a small group of people gathered, mainly police personnel waiting to be dispatched for operational duty. But also, one of our typists, a civilian, was present. She worked at the same office where we were.

"Miss Cunningham, is it you who is going to do the test?" she inquired with a worried look.

"No, it's not me doing the test. I just came to show Thomas how to set up the machine," I replied. "Is everything OK?"

"The driver who will be tested is my brother."

"Oh, OK, sorry to hear that."

I cannot recall if we had any further conversation. Proceeding to the cubicle where the machine was installed, I switched it on. I carried out a diagnostic test to begin with, as the trainer had indicated. The result revealed the fluid needed topping up, but I had no access to the reserve as it was stored in the general office, which was closed for the evening. None of the office key holders was present.

During our training, we were advised that the machine would give a false reading if the fluid needed changing or was not at the correct level.

We were strongly advised that if this happened, we should not proceed with the testing because justice would not be served to the person being tested.

With this in mind, I informed the officers who accompanied the accused man of the situation. They insisted that we should still go ahead with breathalyzing the suspect.

I explicitly stated that it was unfair to the suspect, given that the reading would not be accurate and would be relied upon in court. I advised the officers to go to the next station, where a breathalyser machine was installed. This was about an hour's drive. The officers did not look too impressed by my suggestion.

Upon Thomas reassuring me that he recalled how to operate the machine and given that he was the breathalyzer officer on duty, I handed over the job to him and left for home.

It was for Thomas to decide the course of action to take. He was the one who would have to go to court to account for the reading. The policemen were senior in rank to Thomas, which complicated the situation. I was firm that the machine was out of order and should not be used.

Our training and the installation of the breathalyser machine took place approximately a year and a half prior to the date of this incident. The machine had not been used, so it was not rocket science to understand why it would need servicing.

While I totally sympathized with the family of the deceased and cannot begin to comprehend the pain and agony of losing a loved one, especially to drunk driving, I am also an advocate for a fair trial.

The policemen needed to take the suspect to the next station, but they refused. The following morning, I learnt that the policemen reported to Superintendent Flamingo, the officer in charge of their division, that the breath test was not carried out because I failed to do so. They further alleged that I was good friends with the sister of the suspect, who was an administrative staff, and whom they had seen me conversing with that evening. The officers claimed that my reason for not carrying out the test was to pervert the course of justice.

To verify whether the machine was, in fact, not working, both divisional commanding officers, Superintendent Wilson (my commanding officer) and Superintendent Flamingo, independently decided to have the machine checked. The result confirmed my finding. The machine needed oil, and with the fluid topped up, it worked properly. They even checked and concluded that the fluid was stored in an area locked in the evening. Only general office staff had access to the keys.

Despite this finding, both superintendents conspired to take me down the disciplinary route for not breath-testing the suspect, stating that I was surreptitiously trying to pervert the course of justice.

They compiled a file, including witness statements of persons who were not even at the scene that night, and sent it to the police commissioner's office for me to be charged.

My plea for a fair investigation fell on deaf ears. They did not seek witness statements from persons who were, in fact, present and witnessed what happened.

Their investigation was so flawed it was incomprehensible how the officers' consciences gave them any peace at night.

Additionally, Superintendent Flamingo was the lead officer in the trial of my other disciplinary case. His role was akin to that of a judge. In short, he was like the judge and jury on my cases.

To make matters worse, we did not see eye to eye on some personal issues that I will not discuss here. Therefore, how could I expect to receive a fair trial?

The future of my career was hanging in the balance!

In hindsight, I believe Satan wanted to "sift me like wheat." I reasoned that I was in a desert of vipers, and there was no escaping their venomous bites.

Looking back, I felt like the officers' knees were on my neck, and I was gasping for breath. My shouts met with deafening silence. It was a lonely, dark place to be. My heart ached, and no pain-relief tablets could ease the excruciating agony I felt.

What have I done to deserve this?—A question I often asked myself. Nevertheless, quitting the job was not an option. So, I decided to fight with all the strength I had. But no, not a fight with fists, batons, or guns. A fight in the spiritual realms. A fight on my knees through fervent prayer to God.

I asked God to take on this fight for me. I was too weak, and I could not fight on my own. I knew it was a spiritual battle, even though I did not know much about spiritual warfare then. I felt God was trying to get my attention. So, he allowed me to go through these experiences.

The truth is, I returned to the church, but I was not fully committed. I believe God, in His mercies, saw what I could become rather than who I was at that time. And, man, he really fought for me.

One Friday night, I went to bed stressed out about the cases. Earlier that day, I was served with a paper filed by the commissioner's office. It invited me to respond to the allegations, stating why the preferred (draft) charges should not be made out against me.

The sergeant who served me the paper and whom I later found was not genuine said, "Cunningham, don't give away your defence. Just respond by saying, 'I reserve my defence.'"

I reasoned in my heart: *How will the commissioner know my side of the story if I don't tell it?* Certainly, he would be left with no option but to go ahead and charge me. Therefore, I would have missed my opportunity to have my side of the story heard when deciding whether to charge me.

In a court-of-inquiry disciplinary process, the divisional officer investigates and sends the file to the commissioner's office with what is known as preferred charges. The commissioner's office examines the statements, etc., and decides whether to bring a case. Also, they seek to obtain a response from the person being charged. They instruct whether a court of inquiry is to be convened.

I could not go on vacation leave, sit for a promotional exam, or advance my career in any way. I felt useless and unmotivated.

That night the Lord woke me from sleep to pray about the case. After some time in prayer, the Lord impressed me to "Get up and write."

I began writing about how flawed the investigation was, with no consideration given to the fact that I was off duty when I agreed to help Thomas.

That night I witnessed vividly the power of God at work. Usually, I am a slow writer, but when I put pen to paper, my hands began moving at a speed much faster than I was thinking, as in automatic writing.

I was responding to the allegations in a statement form. It was like someone held my hand and was writing for me. I remembered that when I thought of a point and tried to construct it as a proper sentence. When I checked, I saw that that point was already written.

In a relatively short time, I had a well-prepared statement of approximately five foolscap pages. The layout, structure, sequence of events—everything—was on point! There was no way I could have done that without divine help. It was an amazing experience that baffles me to this day.

That crucial statement, the copy of which I'm still in possession, would become a defining document for my career.

I made a copy and submitted it to the general office to be sent through channels to the office of the commissioner.

The Lord then orchestrated a plan where I would have an audience with the commissioner without having to go through normal channels—that is divine favor!

The protocol to have an audience with the commissioner was snail-paced, winding, and off-putting. Paper files were the order of the day, of course. Typists transcribed handwritten documents in preparation for their intended destination. Unfortunately, many documents ended up in what was known as *File 13*.

In retrospect, my application would have ended up in File 13, aka the trash bin, if I had gone down the normal route. Surprisingly, the practice of victimizing colleagues in this way still continues almost two decades later. For example, I ran across the Jamaican news broadcast's story below.

> *In October 2022, according to the broadcast, the Jamaica Constabulary Force (JCF) high command launched an audit and a misconduct investigation following the discovery of several boxes allegedly hidden by a female inspector of*

> *police. They contained personnel files relating to unresolved disciplinary matters, applications for promotion, and other benefits that had never been submitted. The inspector in question was in charge of administration in that police division. JCF members accused her of deliberately hiding the files over several years. If the accusation was correct, the inspector was intentionally sabotaging her colleagues.*
>
> *The documents were discovered after a check was made on a vacation-leave matter, and the file could not be found. This triggered their eventual discovery in a room to which apparently only that inspector had access.*
>
> The probe is without resolution up to the time of writing this book.

Picking back up with my story, one day, the chaplaincy unit I was assigned to (as one of the peer counsellors) was invited to the commissioner's office. It so happened that I was selected to represent my division. During the meeting, the commissioner paid us a courtesy call—that is, he just popped in to acknowledge the team. One of his assistants was chairing the meeting.

In his brief chat, he issued an open invitation to anyone who wished to have a private consultation with him.

Wow!! Talk about divinely favored! Being in the right place at the right time; yep, that was me.

Without hesitation, I grasped this once-in-a-lifetime opportunity—so overjoyed I wanted to pinch myself to be sure I wasn't dreaming.

Deputy Superintendent Wexford, our Area Force Chaplain, agreed to accompany me to see the commissioner. I invited him for emotional support, as I was truly overwhelmed. I could not believe how fortunate I was. This was an awesome privilege. It's like an ordinary citizen having an audience with the president of the United States without even having to go through a barrage of security background checks.

I might have felt like Albert Abraham Michelson, best remembered for his work on measuring the speed of light. In 1907, he received the Nobel Prize in Physics—the first American to receive a Nobel Prize in the sciences.

The story goes that upon graduating from high school, he applied for admission to the U.S. Naval Academy but was turned down. After traveling to Washington, he made a direct appeal to President Ulysses Grant, who intervened, making it possible for Michelson to be admitted to the academy. Looking back, I could call this opportunity my Michelson moment.

I sat at the commissioner's desk and verbally laid out my case to him. I spoke of my dreams and aspirations within the Force, which had been thwarted by unfair disciplinary actions. I felt like a voice in a wilderness, crying out for justice. Prior to that date, my cries had only been met by ravenous wolves.

The commissioner empathized with my plight, saying he could relate to my situation. He spoke of victimization and engrained institutionalized conduct the Force has not yet managed to arrest.

With that, he promised to personally review my case. He explained that disciplinary cases, especially of the nature of mine, were dealt with by his office but not necessarily by him. However, in this case, he would personally do the review and communicate the outcome.

I walked from the commissioner's office, feeling valued, heard, and re-energized. It was as if the world had lifted off my shoulders.

I reasoned that there was no higher office or tribunal, so whatever the outcome was, I would accept it with grace. I prayed constantly about the matter, and I believe God heard and answered my prayers.

I have learnt to accept what I cannot change. That is, acknowledging when I do not have control over the situation. This is where my faith comes in. The Bible says, "*But let him ask in faith, with no doubting, for he who doubts is like a wave of the sea driven and tossed by the wind. For let not that man suppose that he will receive anything from the Lord*" (James 1:6–7 NKJV)

I trusted that the God who woke me to document my clear, succinct response and then orchestrated this meeting would continue to work on my behalf.

On reflection, it became clearer why it was so vital that I wrote my side of the story. How else would the commissioner know it?

My response statement formed one of the key documents in the commissioner's review of the case.

Several months later, I had heard nothing. Nevertheless, I never doubted the power of God to take me out of a situation.

One evening, Joy, my colleague, and close friend, visited me at home. Knowing my story well, Joy empathized with my plight.

"Cunnie, have you heard anything about your case yet?"

"No, I haven't."

"Are you sure? Have you checked with the general office?"

"Nothing's come back as yet," I responded confidently.

"The other day, I attended a big meeting where the commissioner addressed almost the entire Traffic Division. He made reference to a case, and I am almost certain it is yours."

Joy continued, "Because you and I talked about your case, I feel like I know it quite well. I am almost certain that was the one the commissioner referenced." She pressed on.

"He spoke about a female corporal in Area One who suffered great injustice at the hands of her fellow sub-officers. He did this, making an earnest appeal to treat each other with fairness."

Joy continued, "He said you came to his office requesting that he review your court-of-inquiry case. I am saying 'you' because I know it's you. He was very disappointed about how you've been treated. He said the investigation was totally flawed. He spoke very strongly about your case but did not call your name."

Joy tried earnestly to convince me.

"He said, 'I was alarmed at the injustices she suffered. The female corporal wasn't even on duty when she volunteered to help ensure a driver in a fatal motor vehicle accident was breath-tested. Yet, they wanted her to be charged with perverting the course of justice.

"'There were several officers present at the time she volunteered, yet none of them were asked to give a witness statement, although she had submitted several names. Witness statements were collected from commanding officers who weren't even present. The officer was on her way home with her young son when she went back over a mile to help.'"

Joy then gave the outcome: "Cunnie, the commissioner said he has exonerated you."

"Really, are you serious?"

"Yes, he threw out your case. Check it out."

The scripture says, "*Anxiety in a man's heart weighs it down, but an encouraging word makes it glad*" (Proverbs 12:25 AMPC)—indeed, how this glimmer of hope encouraged my heart.

A sense of peace and calm came over me. *If what Joy just shared was really my case, why then hadn't I received a response?*

Any correspondence would have come by way of the general office—that's the communication protocol.

Have I been sabotaged?

With that probing thought, I spent the evening chilling at the back of my seaside home, which overlooked one of the most magical wonders of the world: the Caribbean Sea, dressed in its blue gown and kindling its own symphony.

At the time, I lived in a rented villa that was once a tourist accommodation. A striking contrast to the humble shack in which I grew up. There weren't many houses along that stretch of shoreline, making the area quiet and intimate.

The large, raised pool at the back of my home was just a few yards above the shore. When the waves were turbulent, they crashed on the retaining wall at the base of the pool, dumping the sea's white foaming crystal water into it. And spraying salt on the house walls.

Still, it was a beautiful and quiet spot, the place to retreat for deep meditation. Policing was a tough job. As for me, having a place to unwind helped in maintaining good mental health. The golden sunset was visible from there, too—a truly breathtaking experience.

As a nature lover, I deeply appreciated the radiating golden glow of the sunset, which ushered an oasis of serenity into my home.

I've always wondered why, before disappearing from the horizon, the setting sun appeared to slowly position itself on top of the calm seas.

Even though I learnt that this is because of the rotation of the earth, still, I will never fully understand it. Imagine the earth is rotating, and we are never tipping over! How awesome is God, the architect of the universe!

In the Bible, it says, "All things were made by him; and without him was not anything made, that was made" (John 1:3 KJV).

If God is so powerful as to create all things, then surely, He can take me out of this horrible pit.

Following on from the conversation with Joy, I greatly anticipated shortly receiving the response from the office of the commissioner.

I waited with bated breath, but let me hasten to tell you weeks passed, and no response arrived. This was in spite of my checking regularly. None, no correspondence. At least, so I thought.

At this point, though not fully understanding what was happening, I trusted God to see me through. In hindsight, I realized that God was teaching me to trust Him more, to get to know Him better. He was preparing me for the work I'm doing now—helping to save lives.

Takeaways

1. Prayer works

When you are going through a difficult situation, pray for guidance and do not give up, even amidst great discouragement. Ask God to give you the strength to endure. You may not fully understand the *what, why, how, when, or where* of your situation, but hold on, nonetheless.

2. God is faithful

Believe the Word of God. In the Bible, God said He would not give us more than we can bear: "*No temptation has overtaken you except what is common to mankind. And God is faithful; he will not let you be tempted beyond what you can bear. But when you are tempted, he will also provide a way out so that you can endure it*" (1 Corinthians 10:13 NIV).

3. Trials help to build our character

One of my favorite writers, Ellen Gould White, says:

> *It is by close, testing trials that God disciplines His servants. He sees that some have powers which may be used in the advancement of His work, and He puts these persons upon trial; in His providence He brings them into positions that test their character and reveal defects and weaknesses that have been hidden from their own knowledge. He gives them the opportunity to correct these defects and to fit themselves for His service. He shows them their own weakness and teaches them to lean upon Him; for He is their only help and safeguard.*[4]

4 Ellen G. White, Patriarchs and Prophets (Nampa, Idaho: Pacific Press Publishing Association), 1958: 129, 130.

Chapter 7
Free at Last

"People will tell you that freedom lies in being cautious," said Robert Frost (he violently shook his head). "Freedom lies in being bold."[5]

Growing up, I felt like a roach in someone's kitchen—constantly on the run, fleeing a swatter, a slipper, or some burst of spritz. As a result, the hands of fear and rejection had a firm hold on me, crushing my every hope, dream, or desire. Timidity, too, was among that crew, paralyzing my every move.

Eventually, I evolved into a warrior, determined to be freed from oppression, intimidation, and degradation.

My stance was like that of David. Facing the great Goliath, he stood—resolute and unswerving! The fact is, adversities taught me to fight—to cower not; persevere, be bold!

It was in the summer of 2004, that time of year again when the Jamaica Police Federation hosted their Annual

---

5 1952 December 13, The New Yorker, Television: Men of Faith by Philip Hamburger, Start Page 167, Quote Page 169, The New Yorker Magazine Inc., New York. (Online New Yorker archive of digital scans).

Joint Conference. An event to which we, the delegates, looked forward.

For some, it was an opportunity to step back from the hustle and bustle of everyday policing to relax in a five-star hotel—you can call it an all-expenses-paid mini-vacation.

For others, it was a time to be immersed in motivational speeches and presentations in the hope of taking back some positivity to the wider membership—like fighter jets returning to base to refuel, then take off again.

Also, there were those whose main focus was to vote for their favorite candidates for the Central Executive Committee—the main highlight of the momentous two-day conference.

That year it was held at one of Jamaica's premier tourist destinations, in the picturesque seaside resort of a tropical coastal town lined with pristine, white sandy beaches and warm turquoise water.

Ocho Rios boasts the world-renowned Dunns River Falls—magnificent cascading waterfalls that empty into the Caribbean Sea. For me, the federation could not have chosen a more charming location.

The police federation is a body within the JCF tasked with the representation of the rank-and-file members—constables, corporals, sergeants, and inspectors. Its duty is to bring matters affecting members' welfare and professionalism to the Commissioner of Police and the Minister of National Security.

The commissioner was not always present at these conferences, but divine providence interceded: that year, he was the keynote speaker.

I sat in the packed conference room, listening to various speakers address welfare matters, policies, and plans while some delegates were busy as bees, canvassing.

Day one rolled away, and day two came into play. Soon it was time for the commissioner's Q&A. This golden lifeline wasn't gonna be missed by any. Suddenly, a day-long, never-ending queue appeared in the center aisle of the room.

One by one, delegates stepped up to an imaginary front line, passionately pleading their concerns. For some, it was a personal issue; for others, issues of the rank and file they represented. Regardless, what was evident was that many members were carrying burdens far too heavy for their shoulders.

The expectation was that delegates make their questions succinct, but as always, there were those whose questions sounded like many pages or even a story out of a book.

I reflected on how privileged I was to have had an audience with the Commissioner—sans rush, sans haste, sans queue, sans wait. There I had spread my case—oppression, victimization, frustration—laying it bare. Even though waiting on the response appeared to have slipped into eternity.

Finally, the queue dwindled to a trickle as synchronized yawning spread across the room. The last delegate stepped up to the imaginary line, voiced his concern, the commissioner responded, and the moderator signaled that Q&A had ended.

Eagerly, I hurried to the elegant dining hall to quiet the rumbling in my stomach. I spotted my friends at an ideal, comfy spot in the exquisite setting, beckoning me to join them. As it was an all-island conference, we were from different divisions and sections. Lots to catch up on.

There was barely any time to soak up the ambience before the many knives and forks began their own orchestral symphony. The smell of sumptuous, authentic Jamaican dishes had me salivating in the line.

Back at the table, my friends and I engaged in some light-hearted banter—frequent bursts of laughter interspersed with tasty food.

It so happened that everyone at our table finished eating and left. I remained. A few were still dining at other tables, though. The waiters were busily cleaning up. Wanting to chill before returning to the conference, I lingered at the table a while longer.

Scanning the hall, who did I see but the commissioner and his entourage advancing? *Finished with lunch, they were exiting adjacent to where I sat*. My head buried deep in my handbag as I rummaged in it; I felt a strong presence close to me.

Looking up, I noticed the commissioner, his staff officer, and two other officers approaching. It looked to me like a state president and his entourage strolling to a meeting on TV.

As they drew closer, my heart leapt; I became uneasy in my chair. *Why were they coming towards my table?*

I looked behind me to see if I was sitting at an exit. But no, I wasn't. Instead, from ceiling to floor, there were only spotless glass walls. Again, I looked right, then left. No corridor, no doors. It then dawned on me that the commissioner was coming to speak with me.

Gasping and somewhat confused, I sprang to my wobbly feet. The group stood right at my table.

Lifting my hand to about the height of my shoulder to salute him as a mark of respect, I suddenly remembered drill training. You must only salute when wearing your headdress—my uniform cap. That day I was in civilian clothing. So, lowering my hand hastily, I stood at attention and gave a slight bow.

"Goo . . . good afternoon, sirs," I gabbled, panicky.

Surely, I've won Mr. Bean's Oscar!

"Good afternoon, Corporal," the commissioner responded in a rather calm and friendly tone.

Aah! The commissioner remembered me, I comforted myself.

"I was looking forward to hearing from you today," he continued.

Unsettled by such words, I became even more disoriented.

Apparently interpreting my confusion, he suddenly interjected, "You came to my office a few months ago, requesting that I review your case.

"Yes, sir, I did."

"Haven't you received my response? Didn't you know you've been exonerated?" he asked with curiosity in his eyes and disapproval in his brows.

"Thank you! No, sir, I haven't received your response. I didn't know."

He continued, "I was expecting you to be in the queue earlier. I was expecting you to say thanks publicly. I wanted members to know that my office gives justice"—emphasizing the word "justice."

"Most members believe we only punish, but I want them to know the other side too."

I felt shivers running through my body, even though the sun had turned up its dial.

Free at last! Free at last! Free at last! —were the shouts in my heart at intensified decibel levels.

Fortunately, that joyous outburst could only be heard by me; if not, the commissioner would think he had a psychiatric emergency at hand.

Turning to his staff officer, the commissioner asked, "In the matter of Corporal Cunningham from Hanover Division, was the outcome sent off to her division?"

"Yes, sir, I'm sure we did," the officer replied.

"Will you make a call to the office and let me know the date that letter was sent out?"

"Yes, sir, I'll do so now."

The officer hurriedly walked to a corner in the same room, where no one was sitting. From there, he made the call.

I remember we continued to dialogue. The specifics of the remaining conversation are blurry. Nevertheless, what I clearly remember was the staff officer returning and confirming that the outcome letter had been sent to my division.

Usually, document delivery was a simple process. A driver was sent to the Commissioner's office in Kingston to drop off and pick up documents. All documents are recorded in a book and signed for. Upon returning to the division, the driver delivers them to the general office, or if the general office is closed on their return, the package is left at the head station until the following morning.

Was I sabotaged? You decide.

"I want you to come back inside and tell the members what happened and what I did for you," the commissioner instructed.

"Wow!"

"But, sir, Q&A is now closed. There was no further Q&A session on the agenda," I reminded him.

"Not to worry," he assured me. "I'll reopen that segment, just so you can speak."

Wow! Is this for real? I thought.

Is the commissioner going to amend the conference agenda just for me?

Just so I can share my story?

Is this really happening to me?

Insignificant me?

His statement left me flabbergasted. I almost collapsed with happiness.

"OK, sir, thank you. I will."

Upon resumption of the conference, true to his word, the commissioner reopened Q&A. Delegates hastily formed a queue again.

I took up my position in the line and waited—at the same time, comforting and encouraging myself. Those days public speaking was not my favorite activity.

Marva, stand up, stand out. Be Bold!

I thought of what to say and how to say it. I didn't know where to start. I wanted to give a TED talk kind of speech; instead, my story was jumbled up in my head.

A voice-over whispered, "Don't worry about what to say. Just open your mouth and start speaking."

I remember stepping up to the front with the commissioner at the podium facing the expectant delegates.

He had a pleasant smile tugging up the corner of his lips. I imagined him feeling like a proud dad at his daughter's university graduation.

After all, by this time, I'd certainly earned an honorary degree from the School of Humanity at the University of Life!

What's my specialty?

Overcoming Adversities!

The moment the commissioner and I were waiting for arrived. All chattering seemed to cease, giving way to a hush. I started speaking—and to my astonishment, my mouth was infused with eloquence.

I heard myself narrating my story, my journey, my truth, my nightmare, my pain, my loss, and now finally—my joy and my gain. At the end of the discourse, I received a loud, almost tumultuous applause amidst statements of affirmation and commendation.

Softening the applause, the commissioner expounded on his disapproval of my unfair treatment, referring to it as incomprehensible. He implored members who were experiencing similar issues to seek an audience with him.

He told them they did not have to go through the usual channels—winding channels, I might add. This was like music to the delegates' ears—a pivotal shift, a turning point we longed for.

During the break, a large contingent of corporals (my rank) approached me, pressing me to put myself forward as a candidate for the Central Executive Committee. They needed strong, bold representation, like what they'd seen and heard that day, they said.

After those two unforgettable days of the conference, I returned to my office, which adjoined the general office. Surprisingly, what greeted me? Make a guess . . . The *elusive* outcome letter dated some weeks prior!

Carefully removing the letter from the envelope and unfolding it, my eyes became affixed to the following words:

"Dear W/Cpl Cunningham,

Please be informed that after careful consideration of the matter, a decision was taken not to prefer disciplinary charges against you."

Once more, I was paralysed with happiness. I could barely conceal my delight. My spirit brightened, and hope bloomed inside me.

Free at last! Free at last! Echoed in my heart again.

I've preserved that letter as a constant reminder of what God has done for me.

Reflecting on my journey—in particular, this experience—took me back to the dispute that *led to my transfer from Kingston to Hanover*. I needed representation from the said body—Central Executive Committee—but, at the time, had none. A different set of personnel was serving then.

Providentially, the commissioner dismissed my second case (the breathalyzer test incident). This is because, at the time I requested the review, the trial regarding the first case (the incident with the female sergeant) had already started.

In the first case, from the *one* instance, they made three disciplinary charges—namely, behaviour unbecoming that of a member of the Force, disrespect to a senior in rank, and unprofessional behaviour,

The outcome was that I would be fined fifteen days' pay—yes, you heard correctly—fifteen days' pay! Five days for each charge.

Following my public exoneration, the police federation agreed to represent me on appeal of the first case. I believe they, too, had a better understanding of the plotting to destroy me.

God would have it that a new commissioner had been assigned—this one I'd never met. Happily, upon my appeal, he rescinded the decision in the award of punishment and directed that all charges against me be withdrawn—*ending all charges against me.*

Looking back, I believe that the Lord ensured that my appeal was heard by a new commissioner to preclude any suspicion or doubt about the decision.

The scriptures say, "The facts of every case must be established by the testimony of two or three witnesses" (2 Corinthians 13:1, NLT).

The two commissioners and their advisors comprised more than three witnesses in my cases. Therefore, the judgment of the commissioners was not only correct but spiritually on point, also.

That's the power of God! When He does something, it is well done.

From this experience, I got a deeper insight into how God increases our faith in His power. I began to recognize God's distinct yet inaudible voice when He spoke with me.

I began to learn His nos and yeses. And sometimes, when He says go and when he says stand still. I developed a sweet relationship with Him, trusting him in times of pain and in times of joy. A relationship that would see big miracles wrought before my eyes.

God says, *"I am the Lord, who opened a way through the waters, making a dry path through the sea"* (Isaiah 43:16 NLT).

He certainly opened a way for me. I had no idea, no clue, how I was going to get past those disciplinary problems. The Lord showed up and made a way. Truly, the Lord did mighty work for me. And He continues to do so up to now.

Isaiah 43:16 tells about the Israelites of old and how God, in a spectacular display, delivered them from Egyptian enslavement in the very presence of their enemies.

I felt like God did a similar kind of thing for me—while not as dramatic.

I am comforted by the fact that the scriptures tell us the power God had then. He still has it now. He is the same yesterday, today, and tomorrow. He does not change. He will deliver us from oppression, exploitation, and persecution. All evil, full stop!

The discipline to which I was subjected was nothing but acts of evil.

Many officers suffered similar experiences—victimization and bullying—impacting not only them but their families, spouses, children, and by extension, the community.

Many who came to know my story were motivated to seek redress via the Commissioner—an office previously known for harsh disciplining only.

I choose to include these experiences in my book, not from a place of bitterness or the naming and shaming of any person or the organization I proudly served for sixteen trying but wonderful years, but from a place of sharing my triumph over adversities by the enabling power of the almighty God, His justice and love.

I believe God allowed me to go through these experiences to show His grace and care, not only for me but for the good of others as well.

During those two years of suffering and oppression, it would have been easy to feel angry and hurt, resentful and disrespectful of those who plotted against me. But I chose to remain calm and humble, trusting God that He would work on my behalf.

I practiced being patient and forgiving, not to fight fire with fire but to be of a teachable spirit and ask God for wisdom on how to act. Humility is strength controlled.

By engaging in self-reflection, I learned valuable lessons from the devastating experiences. I considered where and how things went wrong, asking myself what I could have done differently and taking responsibility for my actions. As such, my resilience muscles developed.

Maya Angelou, the celebrated author, said during an interview, "You may encounter many defeats, but you must not be defeated. It may even be necessary to encounter defeat so that you can know who you are, what you can rise from, and how you can still come out of it."

Though the experience was horrible, I was happy for the lessons I learnt.

Takeaways

If you are experiencing unfair treatment at the workplace, here are some points to consider. This is by no means an exhaustive list.

1. Practice self-care

Unfair treatment at the workplace can be emotionally taxing. Tap into your support networks; they can be, for example, family members, friends, and church leaders. You can also access community support groups. Such groups remind us that we are not alone and that others are experiencing similar issues.

2. Keep a record of the unfair treatment

It is very important that you keep a record of the unfair treatment. This includes email messages, office communications, voicemails, memos, etc. Write down as soon as possible instances of mistreatment. Make sure you record the details and specifics as you remember them. These may become vital in any litigation.

3. Make a report

Seriously consider reporting the unfair treatment to your organization's human resources department, as it will aid in formalizing your complaint. It might help to protect you from further mistreatment. Additionally, it might cause your employer to take steps to address unfair treatment or malpractice.

4. Seek legal advice if you must

Contact an experienced and knowledgeable employment solicitor who can advise you of your rights and the options available.

Chapter 8
New Horizons

Nothing can stop the man with the right mental attitude from achieving his goal; nothing on earth can help the man with the wrong mental attitude.

—Thomas Jefferson

A few years after the events of Chapter 7, in 2004, I switched jobs, eventually becoming a social worker, advocating for abused children in the United Kingdom, my new home, applying the lessons on fairness and justice I myself had learned first-hand. In fact, my own experiences led me to this advocacy. Over ten years passed. Here is how that story unfolded.

Once in primary school, my teacher assigned us to write a story entitled "The Day I'll Never Forget." Contrary to the title, believe it or not, my childhood was such that I was sorely pressed to think of a day I wanted to remember. Now, given its impactful significance on my life, I would definitely write about August 21, 2005, as one of the star-studded, platinum days.

My family and friends, including colleagues, all decked out in their Sunday best, excitedly gathered in Jamaica to celebrate what *shouldn't-have-been*—but nevertheless was—a life-changing occasion, an event hosted at the renowned picturesque Day-O-Plantation restaurant, bar, and wedding venue. Poised in a quiet, uber-secluded hillside, overlooking some of Montego Bay's lush green vegetation, it was formerly a sugar plantation.

If memory serves, a little over a hundred guests mixed, mingled, and frolicked. The swimming pool was alluring, to say the least. Positioned in the center of an open-air lounge, it easily captured the evening rays of the summer sun, causing the glass-clear water to glisten as if it were a properly polished mirror. I am convinced many guests wanted to plunge in. In fact, I had just taken a plunge, but into something much deeper than a swimming pool—my head, my heart, fully swallowed!

Decked out in a stunning off-white, eye-popping, jaw-dropping, figure-hugging, Miss World kinda gown—by my account, of course—complemented with matching gloves, veil, and shiny tiara, I guessed the silent tune on everyone's lips was "*Here Comes the Bride! All dressed in white, sweetly serenely, true love united for eternity!*"

It was my wedding day!

Love, as I saw it then, came looking for me in the form of a British hunk. Smashing down the walls of my barricaded heart and arresting my heart's desire for love, he vowed to be my protector, confidant, motivator, bestie, family leader, and lover—the only man I would ever want or need!

Surely, this time around, I'd got it right—having done my due diligence. And I knew how to sense true love! Not to mention that I'd matured and grown wiser, might I say?

Markedly different than two decades ago. *After all, I'm a police officer, a trained investigator—equipped to detect fraudsters*, I thought. I guess you get where I'm going, don't you?

A male friend of the groom remarked, "What a lucky man! How is it that he came all the way from England and got this lady?"

Well! Looking back, I would say to that guest, "Very good question. Tell me the answer when you figure it out."

I recall that before I began dating my future husband, Andre, my eldest, said to me, "Mummy, I'm getting up in age now; soon, I'll be moving out, and you'll be on your own. You'll need a partner to spend the rest of your life with."

The truth is, my unfortunate experiences in relationships led me to wall up my heart and become career driven, but I was tired of fighting battles in the JCF. It wouldn't have bothered me so much if they were battles with criminals. At least, that's what I signed up to do: "*Serve, Protect, and Reassure without fear or favor, affection or ill will.*"

Frankly, the culture in the JCF had, before my wedding, killed my passion to continue serving. My zeal, my drive to thrive, had waned.

The plan was that we would return to the UK together, but that was delayed due to immigration processes, coupled with the fact that my mother became unwell and I was caring for her. Hence, I didn't reside in the UK until almost two years after I was married.

My husband returned to the UK, and he and I took trips to see each other until everything was sorted out and I was ready to make the move. We were never apart for long periods.

Finally, in May 2007, I embarked upon a totally new chapter in my life: I moved to England—the mother country, the land of milk and honey—albeit, from my limited bird's-eye view, it appeared cows and bees were extinct.

I arrived by way of a nine-hour Virgin Atlantic flight. It afforded us a whole lot of comfort—tucked beside the man I'd vowed to spend the rest of my life with, to love and to cherish, for better, for worse, for richer, for poorer, in sickness and in health, till death do us part, according to God's holy law.

Still, mixed emotions about the move flooded my mind. But in the end, I felt it was right.

Aside from the more serious stuff, moving to Britain gave me the opportunity to fulfill some of my youthful fantasies. As a young child, I'd been fascinated by stories about princes, princesses, castles, and towers. Chief among those fairy tales was "Rapunzel" by the Brothers Grimm.

Rapunzel, an extremely beautiful young girl, lived in a tower from birth, held captive by a cruel witch. The witch visited the tower regularly and called out to Rapunzel a couple of times a day to let down her ridiculously long hair for the witch to use like a rope to climb up.

It so happened a passing prince hearing the witch say the words, saw her climb up. Soon afterwards, he tried it himself and met Rapunzel. Brave prince! The two fell in love, and he started visiting her. The witch caught him and threw him out of the tower, but he and Rapunzel were reunited and lived happily ever after.

Although the story is a fairy tale, it taught me some key life lessons. One is that when something is destined to happen, then no one, regardless of their powers, can stop it. Therefore, we should never give up on our hopes or dreams, no matter how difficult the situation might be or seem.

After fifteen years of living in Britain, viewing those well-fortified, permanently garrisoned fortresses still occupies a prime spot on my bucket list.

Truly, my early days in England were tough, not easy in any shape or form. I believe that even if you enjoy discovering new places, moving from one country to another requires strong mental fortitude, which I had developed.

Coming to England, I had to start life all over! New home, new community, new friends and associates, new culture, new job—basically new everything. At one point, I considered whether I'd made the right decision. I believe it was providence that I had the life experiences I did. It afforded me the resilience needed to navigate settling in.

I became financially dependent on my husband, a very uncomfortable position, I must say. Since joining the police force, I've received a monthly paycheck. I determined how that money was spent: what was and was not a priority. I never had to account for my spending in any way, shape, or form. Becoming financially dependent was challenging on many levels.

Therefore, not surprisingly, my first goal was to secure a job, albeit with limited prospects, because of my immigrant status. To land a job in the government, I needed to live in the country for a minimum of three years with no restrictions on my stay. I didn't meet those criteria.

One day I was alone at home when a newspaper and other leaflets were slid through the letterbox. Usually, I put them aside for my husband. I had no interest in the local news—it was just too foreign, might I say? I was still hooked on Jamaica's news, although it meant traveling several miles to fetch the Jamaican newspapers. Thank God for the increased global use of the Internet. Accessing the news is now at my fingertips. That day I read almost every article in the paper.

I remember seeing an ad for a position at a nursing home near me. Although I hadn't the slightest idea about caregiver work, I was willing to try. The ad stated that no prior experience was needed and I would receive on-the-job training.

Generally, caregiving assistants provide emotional support, assist with daily living tasks, help build relationships and monitor and take notes, among other tasks.

Bursting with heartfelt joy and excitement, I could hardly contain myself. I quickly rang Marie, my only friend in Britain (she had moved from Jamaica prior to me). My friend for over ten years at the time—she is still my friend.

"Marie, Marie, I've seen a job opening in the newspaper."

"What is it?" she asked eagerly.

"Caregiving assistant," I responded.

In a rather flat, off-putting, bubble-bursting tone, she responded, "Sister, you're overqualified for that job."

She must have heard my heart sinking, so she continued in a more comforting tone, "Still, check it out. At least it's a start."

Sharing the job prospect with my husband gave me no comfort either. He was unreservedly unapologetic for his views: "I didn't bring you to Britain to clean people's ass!"

My children, my family—not one of them was excited either. Everyone thought I was taking a *step back* and that I had left a seemingly elevated job position for something less.

Clearly, no one close to me had my vision. But, as usual, I had a determined spirit, unafraid to take a journey all by myself. The truth is, they saw my potential and felt I had more to offer. They didn't want me to demote myself. What they hadn't considered was the journey to get to where they saw me.

Frankly, being eager to integrate into British life and with a passion for helping others meant accepting any job within my skill set. I reasoned that one of the ways to learn about the citizenry and the government's response to their needs was to have firsthand experience. And what better way to do that than by working in the public health sector—given the wait to be qualified for other roles?

In Britain, as in the United States, one way to care for vulnerable individuals and those who need help is moving them into nursing homes, where they receive assistance with daily tasks such as washing, dressing, and eating. An on-site registered nurse deals with medical issues.

Although most healthcare assistants earned the bare minimum wage, I envisaged a greater return than just financial gain. I called these unaccounted-for benefits. Barack Obama, former US president, said, "Focusing your life solely on making a buck shows a certain poverty of ambition. It asks too little of yourself. Because it's only when you hitch your wagon to something larger than yourself that you realize your true potential." I wanted more than an income. I wanted knowledge because knowledge is power, and with power, you can effect change.

God had me on a journey to launch me into my purpose for this era. A journey I hadn't fully understood yet. A journey to become a *game change*r in people's lives. No sooner had I started working in the caregiving home than I acquired an in-depth knowledge of the role of social workers.

I'd heard of the profession previously but didn't understand what the role entailed. Jamaica didn't have an established social work profession then. There was no social care sector, unlike in Britain. Generally, in Jamaica, families look after their aged or vulnerable loved ones.

While working in the nursing home for two and a half years, I often observed social workers visiting clients and advocating for a better standard of care. Intrigued by their power to improve lives, I became interested.

The British Association of Social Workers (BSWA) website tells us, "*Social workers support people to meet their needs and to protect them from harm; they collaborate with family members, friends and others who are also trying to provide support; and sometimes they have to engage with people who have been assessed as posing a risk to others*" [6]

Further to this effect, working in caregiving opened my eyes to the level of abuse individuals can easily face. Often, I'd read about abuse in those facilities, which I find

6 (https://www.basw.co.uk).

disturbing. To witness it can be even more emotionally challenging. I wanted to be a catalyst for change in the lives of the vulnerable.

As a Christian, I learnt that Jesus had compassion, and so should we. He is our master teacher. In John 13:13–15 (NLT), Jesus says, "*You call me 'Teacher' and 'Lord,' and you are right, because that's what I am. And since I, your Lord and Teacher, have washed your feet, you ought to wash each other's feet. I have given you an example to follow. Do as I have done to you.*"

I believe it's always great to assist others in any way we can. To give our time and comfort is a blessing. When we show compassion and kindness to those who are vulnerable, we are practising the merciful attitude that Jesus expects each of us to exhibit at all times. Compassion is a major indicator of Christ's spirit dwelling in us.

To become a social worker, I needed to return to university. Social work is a graduate profession; only those who were appropriately qualified and registered could be called social workers.[7] At that time, international student fees were approximately £9,900, tripling the cost for domestic students. At the then exchange rate of £1GBP = J$135.5, the three-year course would equate to over four million Jamaican dollars, given my international student status—certainly, beyond my affordability.

Discovering that experience in social care was a prerequisite to becoming a social worker; it became clear why the Lord had led me to become a caregiving assistant, even as a complete novice. It looked good on my resume. I was

---

7 "Community: the Heart of Your Social Care Career," 'The government's new legislation will strip social workers of our independence' - Community Care.

fulfilling the requirements for a career I didn't even know I was going into.

I can assure you that it is vital we trust God's lead! He knows the present and the future. He knows what's best for us in every situation. We need to follow His path and trust Him to lead us to success.

Having integrity, compassion, honesty, and kindness, and following your heart regardless of other people's opinions is what I deem success, even though this might not be the world's typical view of success. These traits nourish your soul; their absence makes you cruel, which destroys you.

Some of my greatest life lessons were learnt at the nursing home. I got a better understanding of what it means to care and to be compassionate—priceless teaching that I will forever cherish.

Here are five unforgettable stories illustrating my learning:

1) Mrs. Dorothy, prior to moving into the nursing home, apparently lived a somewhat affluent lifestyle. I can't recall her exact age, but she might have been in her early seventies. She owned a villa on one of the Greek islands, I believe. Usually, she and a girlfriend would spend lots of time there to escape the British winter. It was a great accomplishment: she was living her dream life. Then she started having health problems, leading to poor mobility. She could no longer travel. Having no family support, she was forced to move into a nursing home for the remainder of her days. One day while two of us were attending to Mrs. Dorothy's personal care after a bowel movement, she started sobbing.

"Is something wrong, Mrs. Dorothy?" I asked curiously.

"I can't believe this is what I've come down to," the elegant world traveler lamented.

"What do you mean?"

"Having to have someone clean my butt."

Lost for words, I responded, "Oh, dear!"

"I prefer to die than live like this!" Mrs. Dorothy remarked as she continued to sob.

I tried comforting and reassuring her. "You're no bother to us, Mrs. Dorothy. It's our job to look after you." But she was inconsolable.

"Not that I don't appreciate what you're doing, but I've got no dignity left," she said. "I can't live like this."

Mrs. Dorothy's cries resonated in my heart, lingering for days. I reflected that she spent a fortune acquiring a holiday villa abroad, evidently her pride and joy. But in her last days, what she cared about most—a simple thing like her dignity, her self-respect—she could not obtain by what she had heavily invested in.

Reflecting on the conversation, I thought of this scripture: "No one can predict misfortune. Like fish caught in a cruel net or birds in a trap, so men and women are caught by accidents evil and sudden" (Ecclesiastes:9:12, as explained in Message Version Information).

I believe Mrs. Dorothy did not accept her situation; she wasn't mentally prepared for changes that could come about in later life. Therefore, she found it difficult to cope. But then, some people call England a *nanny state*. There is a stigma about care homes here—most people don't want to go to one. Most prefer to be cared for in their own homes. However, in case after case, some of them find themselves *dumped* there for expediency.

Viktor Frankl, an Austrian neurologist, psychiatrist, and Holocaust survivor, in his book *Man's Search for Meaning*, describes the atrocious cruelties he experienced in a Nazi concentration camp. Also, his observations of other inmates and what he believed was the main way in which they tried to cope. He found that those who could find meaning or purpose in their crucibles were the ones who also appeared to be strong enough to carry on. He discusses how the guards stripped him of his beloved wife, his family, and his clothes. However, he had something left: "Everything can be taken from a man but one thing: the last of the human freedoms—to choose one's attitude in any given set of circumstances, to choose one's own way."

They could not take from Frankl his freedom to choose his attitude. We do not know what is going to happen in the future or even the next minute. We can't control every situation, but we can control how we respond to them.

Among other lessons I learnt from Mrs. Dorothy's circumstances is to be content in whatever situation I am—not to dwell on the past, but instead be grateful for the here and now. And focus on how best to improve my situation moving forward. I learnt that a close relationship with God is key to coping with life's events—sudden, unexpected, or otherwise. God helps us to understand and find meaning in our existence.

2) Mrs. Barbara, a well-polished lady in her early nineties, usually requested to sit in her armchair by the

double-glazed patio door, facing the road that leads to the main entrance gate of the nursing home. From there, she enjoyed reading the papers, watching people arriving or leaving, and squirrels playing hopscotch across the impeccable lawn that bursts with colorful flowers during spring and summer and is snowy white in winter.

Mrs. Barbara loved to be left in her bedroom rather than joining group activities with the other residents. She loved conversing with me, so oftentimes, I popped into her room for a chat, breaking the feeling of isolation. She confided that she owned a house prior to moving into the nursing home but felt forced into moving in.

"What happened?" I inquired.

"Due to my mobility issues and a heart condition, they felt I could no longer live on my own."

Mrs. Barbara gave me insight into her seemingly wonderful life before her husband passed away—in her seventies, approximately twenty years prior. Also, she spoke of her close relationship with her children.

On her birthday and other special days, her children transformed her small bedroom into a sea of flowers and a card factory. Despite the love they lavishly showered on her, Mrs. Barbara wanted to be at home, not there. She only left the nursing home when it was time to occupy her final resting place.

Being from a different culture, it baffled me why her family, who appeared to love her so much, did not comply with her desire. In my culture, the family looks after family members at home.

The most precious gifts we can give our parents are time, love, and care. I learnt to love my aged parents, regardless of the unfortunateness of how I was parented. This experience taught me the importance of listening to my aged parents and respecting their needs. Oftentimes, we want relief from the burden.

3) One evening, I was doing my usual rounds, checking on the patients, when I knocked on the door of Mr. Dennis, a pleasant man in his eighties. I cannot recall any family member ever visiting him. He was unable to speak, so it wasn't surprising he didn't answer my knock. Pushing the door open, I started to greet him when I noticed he had passed away.

Only a few minutes before that, my colleague had checked on him and propped him up in bed, watching the television. He passed away alone, with no family holding his hands. It seemed he had been *dumped* in the nursing home. He spent his last days alone—no family, no friends, only caregivers visiting him.

This experience touched my heart, reminding me that I can't choose when or how I'm going to die. But I can decide how I live my life. We are to love our parents and care for them as they age.

Many adult children are so busy growing up that they seem to have forgotten that their parents are growing old at the same time. You must *"care for your parents with love and respect, for you will only understand their full value when you see their empty chair."*

4) Mr. Cecil was suffering from cancer. A day or two earlier, he had become constipated. Our best efforts to

help him relieve himself fell short, despite the fact he was medicated. While I was attending to him, he said to me, "I don't want to die. I'm not ready to go."

Lost for words, I struggled to reply. His medical chart suggested death was imminent. I felt a deep desire to tell him about Jesus and the hope of eternal life if he accepted Him as his personal Savior from sin.

A *thieves on the cross* kind of moment.

He shared his worry for his wife.

Who will look after her?

"I'm the one who always runs home. I pay the bills and shop. She doesn't know how to do those things."

"Don't worry too much now, Mr. Cecil. She will be OK," I tried comforting him.

I can't remember how we got talking about faith, but we had a conversation about Christ's return and prayer.

Immediately, Mr. Cecil had an aha moment, accepting Jesus as his Savior.

I was surprised when he started praying. He sounded like a seasoned Christian. What became evident was Mr. Cecil's calmness and apparent relief, even though he was still constipated. I felt relieved he was no longer distressed.

Jesus is super cool at lifting our burden when we call on Him! I think it was the following day Mr. Cecil passed away, with his wife and loved ones gathered at his bedside.

5) One morning, I was attending to Mrs. Elaine's personal care when I noticed a big lump in her right armpit. She, too,

was frail and had no speech. No family visited her. My heart was drawn to her.

Following the discovery, she was diagnosed with cancer. Later the tumor burst, leaving a gaping wound big enough to easily fit a cricket ball. The dressing was not able to contain the huge opening, so her body fluid emptied onto the bed. It was like trying to patch a leaky roof in light rain. With great compassion, I attended to Mrs. Elaine's care daily, ensuring she was clean, as dry as possible, and comfortable.

One afternoon I went on shift, hoping to see Mrs. Elaine again, but with some reservations about whether she would still be there.

Walking into the office, one of my workmates remarked, "Marva, we're happy you weren't on shift this morning. Mrs. Elaine passed, and her body has now been taken away. We all know how much you cared for her. It wouldn't have been easy had you been on shift."

I should let you know that we were advised not to be emotionally connected to clients. And to an extent, I do understand the reasoning behind that. On the other hand, keeping one's distance is not easy to achieve. At least, not for me. Let's say I didn't master that aspect of the training well. It was like the advice given to us in police training regarding personal safety: "See everyone as a criminal until they have proven otherwise!"

Frankly, in the recesses of our hearts, we know that caregiving is an expression of the undeniable fact that we are all connected.

I didn't even notice that other people saw how emotionally connected I was to Mrs. Elaine. I did for her what I would like someone to do for me had I been in her position. What I did for her, I did for me because I had learnt patience and attentiveness, which gave me joy and peace. The experience made me *human*. These cases and many others taught me two key skills: humility and compassion—skills that would become key in the career God was positioning me for.

Additionally, helping others made me grasp the real concept of the frailty of us humans and the fleeting nature of life. Putting life into perspective, seeing it for what it really is. Recognizing we are here today and gone tomorrow. Therefore, we should live each day to its fullest.

Not only did the role of caregiving assistant help me to form some good friendships, but also to get perspective. The experience also helped to build empathy for how uncomfortable it can feel to be vulnerable and ask for help.

The Lord knew I needed these foundational lessons, equipping me to practice well the profession he would later have me enter.

The experience made the scriptures jump off the pages of the Bible into my heart, might I say—especially the counsel from King Solomon, one of the wisest men who ever lived:

Honor and enjoy your Creator while you're still young,

Before the years take their toll and your vigor wanes,

Before your vision dims and the world blurs

And the winter years keep you close to the fire.

In old age, your body no longer serves you so well.

Muscles slacken, grip weakens, joints stiffen.

The shades are pulled down on the world.

You can't come and go at will. Things grind to a halt.

The hum of the household fades away.

You are wakened now by birdsong.

Hikes to the mountains are a thing of the past.

Even a stroll down the road has its terrors.

Your hair turns apple-blossom white,

Adorning a fragile and impotent matchstick body.

Yes, you're well on your way to eternal rest,

While your friends make plans for your funeral.

Life, lovely while it lasts, is soon over.

Life as we know it, precious and beautiful, ends.

The body is put back in the same ground it came from.

The spirit returns to God, who first breathed it

(Ecclesiastes 12:1-7 MSG)

Usually, on my route to work, I drove past a housing development under construction. Somehow each time, I felt the urge—like a magnet against steel—to turn into the site. Resisting the urge, I reasoned I couldn't afford any of those beautiful houses, so there was no point in viewing them.

Looking at my circumstances—I had recently come to the country, earning a meager salary, and my husband had other plans—it would be wasting time to even look at the houses. Somehow, I continued having that magnetic pull towards the estate.

One day, unable to resist, I found myself on the beautiful, picturesque, serenely breathtaking sight. I started visualizing myself as one of those homeowners.

Then in October 2007, parking at the front of one of the houses on display, I imagined my Christmas tree in the bay window, announcing to the community the birth of Christ. I saw myself shoveling snow from the drive and the walkway leading to the white, partially glazed entrance door. My begonia flower bed beneath the same window, shouting *spring is here!* Not to mention my neatly mowed striped lawn, arrayed in the summer months' garb. I didn't want my dream to end.

I knew I needed to commit this desire to God, who promised not to withhold anything good from us.

The housing market ballooned, making the odds against me securing a mortgage even higher. But I persisted, nonetheless, determined to defy the odds.

May I just hasten to tell you that four days before Christmas that same year, I stood in the bay window of said house, beside my Christmas tree, with all the trappings I could find to decorate, announcing our residency: *We've made it home in time for Christmas!*—the flickering lights seemed to say.

In January 2008, less than three weeks from the date I moved in, the topic that dominated the news was the recession.

Recession, recession—Britain hits recession. The greatest since World War II, the analysts said.

It resulted in banks withdrawing several mortgages and repossessing many homes. Despite my niggardly financial standing at the time and what was happening around me, God kept my mortgage and home intact.

That's the awesome God we serve!

Fifteen years later, I'm living in said house. I no longer put up Christmas trees, reminding of Christ's birth. Instead, I try making the way I live, the things I do, and the words I speak a testament to the birth, death, and resurrection of Jesus Christ—even though I don't always get it right.

I recall that some time ago, one of my neighbors, renting his house, used me as a drawing card. He'd tell his applicants, "She is the nicest neighbor one could ever have." To be honest, I didn't really think of myself like that. I was just being myself—if you know what I mean.

With hindsight, I believe becoming a homeowner was partially my reward for the care I gave to the vulnerable at the nursing home. There was no way I should have been able to buy and maintain a brand-new house, given the chaos happening in my life at that time.

That was truly defying the odds!

Thank God for my humble beginning. To use one of my mother's favorite sayings, I "stayed on the crooked and cut straight." Meaning use what you have to do the impossible, especially when resources seem to be scarce. Truly, this saying evoked a feeling of being able to accomplish the seemingly impossible, causing my actions and thoughts to be in sync, accomplishing my desires.

As if battling a recession didn't bring enough challenges of its own, another revelation rocked my entire world!

What other odds did you defy? I hear you ask.

For a long time, I suffered in silence, too ashamed to tell anyone. I felt deceived, betrayed, cheated, robbed, despondent, and lost.

My seductive hunk decided to *play the field*. No wonder he hadn't minded so much when I was living in Jamaica. Very convenient.

Now, as he told his concubines and himself, "In this recession, there might be a scarcity of some goods and services, but I'm available in abundance!"

My marriage became so crowded I could hardly breathe or think. Again, I felt my world come tumbling down.

Not another disaster! I screamed in my thoughts, still fragile.

Not another battle to fight!

This can't be happening to me in a foreign land.

How I did not see this coming is beyond me!

I'm a Christian and a former cop.

"These things shouldn't happen to women like me," one might say. At least, that's what I'd thought.

How could I have been so wrong?

However, God stood as my safety net, as always.

Be sure to grab a copy of my next book, revealing intimate details of my struggles to navigate and survive that devastating marriage.

Moving on, at the height of a recession bringing with it major job losses in Britain and worldwide was a worrying time for many. Nevertheless, God kept me calm and showed me how to carry on.

He had me on the move—truly defying the odds, as I kept marveling at this truth.

Deciding to chart a path on my own, separated from my husband, I was successful in a job application in a residential children's home. It paid far more than I'd been earning at the nursing home, putting me in better financial stead. However, I was dying on the inside.

Numerous seeping boils took up residence on my face, revealing the depth of my emotional struggle and my loneliness.

How easy to give up and throw in the towel. But I kept focus, using my situation as an accelerator to push forward. Notice the word *chose*. Recognizing my broken marriage could push me either backward or forward, I *chose* the direction. Determined not to be sidetracked. I learned to manage my emotions.

I read a quote that says, "It's not stress that kills us; it's our reaction to it." Therefore, I refused to become angry and bitter, reasoning that God has given me charge over my emotions. I was determined not to mismanage them by giving dominion to the devil.

God admonishes us: "*And don't sin by letting anger control you. Don't let the sun go down while you are still angry, for anger gives a foothold to the devil" (Ephesians 4:26–27 NLT).*

Instead, I allowed the peace of God to *guard* my mind. You might ask, "Guard you from what?"

From acting impulsively, selfishly, or maliciously—from acting in any way that would result in loss and regret.

In my new job, I saw what happened to children placed in the Health and Social Care system—an experience useful to me if I was to become an excellent social worker.

Vulnerable children, in my opinion, just needed love—in good measure. The scriptures say love covers a multitude of sins, and I believe I was in the right place at the right time to lavish love upon those children, going above and beyond to meet them at their point of need.

To my workmates, I was simply good at my job. But in my heart, I was pouring love upon them.

Giving sympathy, not grudgingly but liberally by kindly words and acts, having a kind, unselfish interest in them, I was trying to make their path easier. I poured out on them what I wanted for myself—love and affection. As I did so, my own problems, as gigantic and monstrous as they were, shrunk into insignificance by comparison. There's something about helping others. I believe it provides a natural sense of accomplishment.

I recall working the night shift in one of the homes where staff struggled, settling Anabelle (not her real name) into bed. Her dysregulation impacted the other children to the extent that the entire house became uneasy.

It was a tough job. Sometimes to help settle the children into bed, additional staff had to be called in. Staff felt Anabelle needed a psychological assessment.

I said she needed good doses of love and affection.

One night while I sat in her bedroom, trying to help her go to sleep, she asked me to scratch the bottom of her feet. I did so gently and tender-heartedly. This surprised her; she thought that no staff would touch her sweaty, smelly feet.

In a short time, she fell asleep. Each night on shift, I would do the same. Once she settled down, the entire house did, also. The staff asked how I got her to sleep. I explained the power of touch. In essence—love in action.

Later it happened that one of the psychologists' recommendations was that she be touched; for example, allowing her to sit on our laps. Even without being a psychologist, it didn't take rocket science to see that this child needed love.

In the UK, when vulnerable children and teens are unable to live with their families, in most cases, the local authority becomes corporate parents, sharing the responsibility for making most of the important decisions regarding the children's welfare and upbringing.

The main reason for children going into the social care system is neglect or abuse. Social workers play a major role in the decision of whether to place children into the care system. Some of the decisions could have been different if the families had had adequate early intervention.

Residential social care experience is invaluable in a social work career. On reflection, I see that God had set me up!

That job was just preparation for the job God really had in mind for me—if I stayed faithful. Looking back, I can see how God directed my steps. The Palmist says, "The Lord directs the steps of the godly. He delights in every detail of their lives" (Psalm 37:23 NLT).

I garnered certain qualities needed for my next job. Things like character development—patience, gratitude—and knowledge. I learnt social care laws, effective communication skills, and working successfully with challenging children, teens, and hard-to-engage parents.

I can assure you that when you're led by God, no experience is ever wasted because "God causes everything to work together for the good of those who love Him and are called according to his purpose for them" (Romans 8:28 NLT). God knows what He is doing; we must trust Him. He uses every experience to bring about His will and fulfil our joy.

In 2010, believing this was how God was leading me, I applied for admission to the social work degree program at two universities.

To my great disappointment, I was refused by both. My test scores weren't high enough. It was evident I didn't know much about a key social-care policy. This was the Children's Act 2004, the Every Child Matters Act, designed to protect the well-being of all children from birth, not failing any.

Deflated and unmotivated, I now started reasoning that social work probably wasn't for me.

"Just accept it; you're a failure," Satan taunted me.

"Can't you see everything around you is failing? Without your husband's support in this foreign land, you won't make it."

It's like failure has me bound up, properly chained! I thought I had broken up with failure and rejection. I didn't know they accompanied me to England.

For a while, I contemplated accepting defeat. But God connected me with Winsome, a spiritual mother and sister who attended my church. Also, Marie, my friend.

Those two ladies saw in me what I had lost sight of—the strength and tenacity I didn't know I had left. They made sure I reapplied for entry to university that same year. However, the only university that had an opening for the course I needed (a social work course) was De Montfort in Leicester, approximately an hour's drive away. And much longer during rush hour. Alternately, there was a two-and-a-half-hour train commute. Whichever way I chose to travel, if I was successful in my application, taking the course meant a long commute, at least three days per week.

One of my workmates remarked, with a rather ridiculous facial expression, "Marva, are you crazy? Do you know how far Leicester is from here? You can't travel to a university far away!"

"You can't . . ." and "You're crazy" kept echoing in my head like a snoozing alarm clock. Satan's strategy of defeat, I called them—coming directly from his throne, masked in my workmate's voice.

I remember my instant response was, "One of the things I like about Britain is its excellent transport system. You can get a bus to almost anywhere in the country. Where there is no bus route, there is a train route, taxi, or private commute. I will get to Leicester each day!" On reflection, I should have added by God's grace, as my life is in His hands.

Her challenge propelled me to push harder toward the seemingly impossible achievement. I was determined to defy the odds!

Upon applying, receiving an invitation for an interview at De Montfort University clearly indicated to me I was on the right path. My hope was not lost. I prayed like any good Christian should, prepared well, and showed up on time. Satan tried his utmost to defeat me, making the interview most grueling.

Nevertheless, I walked away that evening, bursting with confidence that I had smashed it.

Without being big-headed, receiving an email the following day offering me a place on the course starting October of that year came as no surprise.

I'm a true believer that what's yours is yours; no one can take it away from you!

It is said, supposedly by Henry Ward Beecher, that our *best successes often come after our greatest disappointments.*

That's me, for sure.

Although I'm fortunate to have traveled to many places by train, my daily commute to and from university for those three eventful years was particularly unforgettable for its breathtaking scenery in the countryside.

Commuting can be boring, but I purposefully and determinedly made the most of the journeys, using the time to catch up on reading and progressing through my assignments. Not a minute wasted!

When I was not reading, I would catch up on messages, return phone calls, converse with family and friends, listen to soothing music, or plan my day—thus wiping away any stresses. By the final year, the journey seemed so much shorter, even though the route remained unchanged.

In July 2013, walking across the graduation stage was quite a surreal moment. The corner of my lips extended almost to my earlobes, placing my ivories on display in what seemed permanent that afternoon.

Joy flooded my heart.

As I shook hands with the chancellor, grasping my degree, I felt it was mission accomplished!

I knew I wasn't just holding a degree.

I'd grasped a world of amazing opportunities. Not just for myself or my children but for every vulnerable child and family I would work with. Affording them a better way of life.

Working to safeguard was definitely my speciality. A challenging but rewarding area of social work. I developed a heart for serving others from not just my own experience but from on-the-job experience. I was determined to make a difference in people's lives.

Not being able to access tuition fees from Student Finance due to having a previous degree, I had to work part-time while studying. Many evenings I became so overwhelmed by my situation—work, long travel, university assignments, and dealing with a broken marriage. My train journeys became my place of solace as I sobbed and washed my troubles away.

Not only did the school of hard knocks teach me many lessons, but also, I became passionate about helping children and families improve their lives.

I read an article that says, "When God gives you a vision, be prepared to cry over it because every vision comes with a price tag. The road to success is through tests and trials."

God promises that "*They who sow in tears shall reap with joyful singing"* (Psalms 126:5 AMP). "*Everything in life has a season*" (Ecclesiastes 3:1-8). There is a season for weeping and a season for reaping. When you make the most of your seasons, you become *"like a tree planted by the rivers of water, which yields its fruit in season*" (Psalm 1:3 NIV).

You must know your season and maximize it. You can't reap when it's sowing time, and you can't sow in reaping time.

Apples don't grow all year round.

Setting your mind on a goal is the easy bit; keeping it set is tough. It calls for a daily commitment. Anybody can make a start, *but you need the heart of a finisher.*

I became the social worker I wanted to be according to the purpose which God has for my life.

The road was rocky, but with God, I got there. Along the way, I met some guardian angels who kept watch over me, protecting me from *predators* in the system. One such angel is one of my former managers, whose testimony is in part two of this book.

Now I work extensively with children and families, advocating better lives for them.

Seeing hundreds of children's lives transformed—sometimes through grave difficulties, including neglect, abuse, sexual and criminal exploitation, homelessness, mental health, drugs and alcohol misuse, and domestic violence—just to name a few—gives me great joy.

Now God has set me up in such a way that I no longer go looking for jobs—they're always on a relentless hunt for me. I now have the privilege of negotiating my pay rate prior to starting a job contract.

Therefore, no longer do I feed from the crumbs that fall from the government minimum-wage table. I'm able to throw a lavish banquet—by my standards, of course!

That's the power of God!

Takeaways

1. Have the right mindset

It is vital that we have the right mindset to shift things in our lives that might hold us back. We all have *issues* that we struggle with, some of which are not of our own making. Issues we have inherited from our parents and our connections. Things like abuse, anxiety, fear, addiction, and so on. We can break destructive connections, family and otherwise. God, our maker, wants us to live an abundant life. Even if we are experiencing abuse and other dysfunctionalities, we can do so.

2. There are no impossibilities with God

By ourselves, we are powerless to overcome life's difficulties, but by God's grace, we can. We can turn our mess into a message, our test into a testimony, and our trial into triumph. We can't do anything about our yesterday, but we can change our tomorrow for ourselves and our children.

3. Hold to that mindset no matter what

God gives us "*strength that endures the unendurable and spills over into joy*" (Colossians 1:11 MSG). Moving from a caregiving assistant to a children's residential caregiver (while reeling from a broken and devastating marriage that should have destroyed me) to a children's social worker only happened by first having the right mindset. I hold the firm belief that my actions will influence the outcomes of my personal circumstances, so I acted purposefully, determined to show my children that they can defy the odds.

Trust God!

Part Two

The Impact of Defying Odds

Overcoming poverty is not a task of charity, it is an act of justice. Like slavery and apartheid, poverty is not natural. It is man-made and it can be overcome and eradicated by the actions of human beings. Sometimes it falls on a generation to be great. You can be that great generation. Let your greatness blossom.

—Nelson Mandela

The Impact, Firsthand

Defying odds is succeeding where most people think you would fail. But having read the previous chapters of this book, I trust you're not just having a look. Instead, you've learnt the tune of my song, and you're singing along because you are convinced that—You Can Defy the Odds!

It has always been my joy to share my story and impact others with my message. This is one of my divine appointments: to empower others who have had similarly adverse life experiences—persons who feel handicapped by their circumstances and are stuck in them.

God has empowered me, through adversity, to empower others. As wisely summed up by a friend, "My teenage challenges were like throwing kitchen compost in the garden one year, and the following year reaping the nourished plants of the bountiful yields."

It is a joy to serve in my God-ordained purpose.

"All praise to God, the Father of our Lord Jesus Christ. God is our merciful Father and the source of all comfort. He comforts us in all our troubles so that we can comfort others. When they are troubled, we will be able to give them the same comfort God has given us" (2 Corinthians 1:3-4 NLT).

Here are a few of the testimonials from persons whose paths have crossed mine:

1. Shauna, an auditor, wrote:

I met Marva in college. Marva was one of two police-women in our class on leave from the police force. I was sixteen years of age, had just graduated from an all-girl boarding school, and had lived a very sheltered life, having had very little interaction with the opposite sex.

Marva had such a warm and caring nature, so much so that when a young man who did not appreciate my rejection of his advances came on the school campus with nefarious intentions, I immediately ran to Marva for help. Marva, along with the other officer, went outside the class to speak with him. I do not know what was said, but I was very relieved and thankful when he left.

Marva's guidance and protection continued at the university. When she found out my application for boarding on campus had been rejected, she stated that there was a space in her room and was adamant I was going to get it. We went to the office that day, and through Marva's charm and power of persuasion, I received that placement. Marva saved me from having to commute from what we later found out was a very dangerous neighbourhood in the city of Kingston.

I used to tell Marva that she would be an excellent teacher. I remember attending accounting classes, and no matter how hard I tried, I could not grasp the concept the lecturer was trying to impart. I gave up. The night before our exam Marva inquired as to why I wasn't studying. Having found out that I had given up, she set about to prepare me for the exam. I was so surprised that it was the same course because Marva made it seem so easy. I aced the exam the following day! I would not have graduated from university with honors without Marva's help.

Marva and I kept in touch after university; she invited me for a visit. To my mother's dismay, I never returned home. Marva persuaded me to stay with her and even helped me find a job. She took me to the bank and persuaded the operations manager to give me an interview, and I received my first job. Today I am an auditor in a government department in North America.

I affectionately refer to Marva as my big sister, as that's what she's been to me for over twenty years. She's loved, protected, guided, and taught me so much that I can never thank her enough or repay her.

Thank you, Marva.

2. Zuwena, a pharmacist, wrote:

I have known Marva for over two decades. We met at the Montego Bay Community College in 1997, where we were both pursuing a diploma in Business Administration, and we have kept in touch over the years. When we attended college together, Marva was a non-traditional student, had already been in the workforce for years, and was also a mother. Most of us in the same class were fresh out of high school, bright-eyed and bushy-tailed, with no real-life experience.

Marva taught us a lot of life lessons. I can vividly remember a group of us listening to Marva's stories about her early days in the police force, where her morals and values were put to the test, and she often had to stand up for what was right, despite the implications.

Being around Marva was synonymous with being safe. I remember one holiday when we were in our final year of university, we wanted to go home to spend time with our family, and Marva decided to drive home to Montego Bay along with three other students and me.

On the treacherous journey home through the hills of Mount Rosso, the car developed some mechanical issues just as soon as it became dark. My usual reaction was to panic because, back then, cell phones were not common.

I felt safe because I knew I was with Marva; the feeling is like a child feeling safe around their parents. I remember us pulling up to the side of the road into someone's yard, and Marva went to ask for help.

I am not surprised Marva is currently in the field of social work because she has a caring and nurturing personality.

Marva is truly an inspiration to me because she proves that you can achieve anything if you put your mind to it.

I wish her story to be told to every young mother in Jamaica because it is truly inspirational.

3. Shana, a support worker, wrote:

I met Marva through the Lucea Police Youth Club. I was the Assistant Secretary, then the Secretary.

Marva's leadership skills taught me a lot about life and its challenges.

I recall one of our accomplishments as a club was an outreach program at the Copse Boys Home. We had to solicit both *cash and kind* from business owners and individuals in the community in order to provide transportation, food, personal items, etc., for the children at the home. The whole process was a great experience for me. I learnt to care for others, especially the less fortunate.

Marva is a determined lady who rises above any difficult situation or challenge. She always reminded us to do good, no matter what—to be a go-getter. She was always praying and sharing her faith. She wanted the best for herself, her children, and everyone with whom she came in contact.

4. Andrew, a policeman, wrote:

Many young men are caught up in a life of crime by circumstances and not by will. There are many things that have faded from memory with time. However, escaping degrading and turbulent life circumstances remains etched on the forebrain of Andrew Matherson.

A true story of how his life was saved by none other than the one who saved it.

The runaway boy had no desire to be a twenty-four-year veteran of the Jamaica Constabulary Force, but he is. I lost my compass back home.

There was one person, though, that possessed something different from the others. That person was not driven by an attachment due to blood ties.

That person was followed up by an all-inclusive approach to problem-solving. To ease your curiosity, here is how it all started.

My father died when I was fifteen years old. I was told by many that I was now the man of the house. I was to take over where my father left off, and I believed it. I wanted to run the house as a child.

Furthermore, in my immature understanding of life, my mother was not as eloquent, educated, or smart as I was. Unlike Dad, who was able to and did check my books and ensured that I did the work teachers gave me, Mom was less concerned. This caused many tense moments at home, and there was the constant struggle to be the man I wanted to be but did not have a say about it. Constantly, Mom and I argued because she wanted to lead me, but as far as I knew, I was a man, and my opinion mattered.

I became a member of the Police Youth Club in Lucea sometime in the early 1990s, maybe '91 or '92. At that time, one of the leaders was an officer named Cunningham. Miss Cunningham was the name I called her. She wasn't like many officers whom I feared. She was personable. She was firm at times but gentle on other occasions. She commanded my respect, and many of the other clubites gave her the same respect I did. I cannot recall one that did not.

Fast forward to an evening I had an argument with my mother. I did not use swear words, and I was not physically abusive, but I am told that my silence can be deafening, and when I do speak, my words can be piercing. I had had enough; I could take no more of my mother's badgering, mistreatment, and abuse. I did not pack a bag, and I did not know where I was going, but one thing was for sure, I was leaving, and I was not returning. I was a man and should be treated as such.

As I walked along the main road, many people passed me. Some greeted me, and I feigned a response. The tears escaped my eyes as I walked. I constantly dried them, but a wave of unimaginable things went through that tiny head of mine, pushing them onto my face.

When the car stopped near me, I did not care or even want to speak. My heart lifted when the voice I heard said, "Andrew." The way my name was called that alone made a difference. It was followed by, "Are you OK?"

I responded, as I had many times before on that day, "Yes, I am OK."

"You don't look like the Andrew I know; talk to me; tell me what's wrong."

I told you before that memory loss is affecting my writing. I do remember the conversation because it meant so much to me. I wanted to feign a feeling, to make up a story, but Miss Cunningham was so nice to me, a contrast from what I encountered earlier. I tried to open my mouth, but instead, tears came washing down my face, and only strange sounds came from my mouth. Don't ask me what those were, for they have been erased from my memory.

I cannot recall whether Miss Cunningham was in plain clothes or not, but I remember her saying she just needed to stop by her house for a moment and that I should wait on her. She took me to her house nearby. She must have because had she done anything else, I would have disappeared. Had she let me out of her sight for any length of time, I would have been gone. She spoke with me for a little while, then told me she was taking me back to my home and would talk to my mother. She did. How she got me there—you can figure that out on your own. I am of no help.

I recall Mommy allowing Miss Cunningham and me into her bedroom, away from everyone else. Miss Cunningham said we were going to talk, and my mother (who must have been boiling hot inside and regretting seeing the boy who had just walked out of her life come back to her with a total stranger) let us into her bedroom.

I know my silence must have been deafening because Miss Cunningham encouraged me to write if I did not want to talk. I wrote. I addressed my mother in writing. She did not quarrel as in other times. She spoke to Miss Cunningham and me. Yes, she spoke to me, not quarreling.

For the first time, I felt like I had a voice, and what I said mattered to Mom. We were there for a very long time. I cannot say how long, but it was to me a lifetime. It was at that moment, with the three of us there, that Mom and I had a real conversation. That was the moment that changed my life. From then on, if there was any issue that I could not speak about, I would write to Mom, and she would respond.

Today my mother and I are inseparable. Thank you, Marva Cunningham-Hyatt. I realize that you cared. You could have just passed me by. You were on your way home, and insignificant me needed not to be a bother to you. I didn't even see you. Therefore, if you had done nothing, I could not have held it against you. You were able to not only command the respect of youth club attendees, but you were tactful enough to win my mother's trust. I thank you every day in my heart and sometimes publicly as I lecture to the youth across Jamaica, encouraging them to stay on the path to prosperity and not spiral into atrocious activities that undervalue their character.

To Marva Cunningham-Hyatt. I am forever grateful for changing my direction and for setting me on a path that has impacted society positively.

Andrew Matherson was enlisted in the Jamaica Constabulary Force on September 10, 1997, and is today a detective serving in the narcotics division. He is one of the leading Dangerous Drugs Demand Reduction lecturers for the unit that serves Western Jamaica.

He is also an elder at the Seventh-day Adventist church in Lucea, a three-time parish champion in the Jamaica Library Service National Reading Competition, and has many more accolades, trophies, and certificates. But none of them, he says, "would have been achieved had it not been for the intervention of someone who saw beyond the façade, intervened by choice, and purposely impacted me in a positive way. Thanks a million."

5. Veenita Jassel, Social Work Team Manager, wrote:

I have known Marva since 2012 when I worked in a Local Authority Child Protection Team as a senior social work practitioner. She was assigned as my student social worker; I was her practice supervisor. She was a delight, as she was eager to learn and motivated to do well. She was full of energy and positivity, which is always a welcome addition to a very busy social work team.

I watched her develop. She was always inquisitive and wanted to learn as much as possible. She reflected on her learning and developed her own style. Marva has always been open and honest, and her feedback was always welcomed. At the time, she was living in the UK with her youngest son. She worked on the weekends whilst on placements, and her determination to succeed was obvious. I was like a proud parent when she passed her placement, and we said we would stay in contact.

I always wondered what made her the unique individual she is. I only knew her recent history from the ad-hoc discussions about family life and balancing studying and working.

Our paths crossed again in Family Court years later when Marva was a senior social worker. We spoke about working together again one day. That opportunity arose in 2017 when I was managing a team, and Marva came to join it. She dealt with challenging situations and pressures from frontline child protection.

It was another proud moment when Marva found her love and married. I was honored to speak at their wedding in front of her children, family, and friends. It was during this period that Marva shared her personal journey with me, that formed the early chapters of this book.

Whilst I didn't know what her experiences were, I did know that she had experienced adversity and had resilience and, most of all, faith. This was because I saw how she approached challenges around her. If a difficult situation at work needed to be resolved, I knew Marva could handle it as she had an inner strength.

When she told me that she was writing a book, I knew it was what she needed to do next in her life/career. There are sad moments in her story where you can feel her disappointment and pain. However, this is alongside her joy and happiness when she has overcome obstacles.

It takes bravery to share your personal experiences and innermost thoughts, but I know that Marva has reached a place in her life where she is ready to pass on her experiences so others can learn life lessons and take inspiration.

Acknowledgments

I thank God for His divine leadership and blessings as I wrote this book. This was only made possible by Him, my God, Creator, and Saviour. To you be all the glory, honor, and praise. My prayer is that this book will reach thousands of hands and transform hearts and lives for your Kingdom and glory.

When I set out to write this book, I never envisaged the journey on which it would take me—a lengthy roller coaster but more rewarding than I could ever have imagined.

Writing this book presented the opportunity to reflect on the many battles fought and how God miraculously made me triumph over adversities whilst healing me in the process. Even throughout this project, I was still defying many odds, making me more determined to complete it.

God has positioned some key people to assist me on my journey. Recognizing I cannot name them all, I would like to acknowledge a few here:

I owe a debt of gratitude to my amazing husband, Winston, for his continuous encouragement and support of my writing. Early mornings, when I would rather sleep in, he was like my constant alarm clock, ensuring I was penning thoughts. At times when this project took precedence, his patience and understanding never waned.

To Andre and Adrion, two of my wonderful sons and informal editors, without your motivation and support, this book would not be in print. Andre, each time I sought to put words to paper and was gripped by the thought of holding back on some of the unpleasant experiences, I remembered your advice: “Mummy, go deeper. Tell your story. Don’t be afraid. Don’t hold back.” My three sons, thank you for your inspiration.

To Winsome Griffiths and Marie Hemmings, my besties—rather, mum and sister, respectively. Thank you for encouraging me to write this book. You saw the author in me I didn’t see in myself. I’m forever grateful. You’re like guardian angels.

To Pastor Richard Brooks, one of the former pastors of my church. Thank you for your encouragement, spiritual guidance, and leadership during my early years as one of the heads of departments at Walsall Seventh-day Adventist Church. Your leadership has helped to solidify my spiritual foundation. Also, thank you for proofreading my manuscript, thus ensuring it is biblically on point.

To Percival Bramble, my prayer buddy, orator, informal coach, and friend, words cannot express my depth of gratitude for the many hours you dedicated to working through my manuscript with me—pulling the stories out of the deep recesses of my mind. Thank you, thank you, thank you. May the Lord bless you immensely in return.

To Dr. Nadine Collins, my former coach from the Elite Book Coaching Experience, I thank you for your guidance and mentorship. To my fellow authors and the sisterhood forged in that program—you have been a big blessing.

A special thank you to Margaret Harrell, my extraordinary editor and, if I might add—coach! You are truly inspirational, encouraging me every step of the way. You went above and beyond to ensure I kept moving the project along. Your expertise—marked by your professionalism, your keen eye for details, and your creative mind, coupled with your extreme patience—has transformed my feeble, scattered thoughts into the masterpiece this book is today. I thank you.

To the dedicated and resourceful team at Self Publishing.com who have taken this book to publication, I'm indeed grateful.

Finally, to all my family, friends, and spiritual leaders who encouraged and supported me in one way or another, ensuring I publish this book; from the depth of my heart, I thank you.

URGENT PLEA!

Thank You For Reading My Book!

I really appreciate all of your feedback and
I love hearing what you have to say.

I need your input to make the next version of
this book and my future books better.

Please take two minutes now to leave a
helpful review on Amazon letting me know
what you thought of the book

Thanks so much!

-Marva Hyatt

Printed in Great Britain
by Amazon

31210636R00115